"*Scripture and Scrubs* is anchored in faith and resonates with purpose. With thoughtful reflections, real stories, and grounded in truth, the authors provide practical application on how to authentically serve and live for Christ while working in healthcare. This book is for everyone from students embarking on their journey to experienced professionals seeking to reignite their passion. I am deeply blessed by this work and confident it will be a blessing to others."

—**Betty Allen**, chair of nursing, University of Mount Union

"This book is a must read for all Christian healthcare professionals on the frontlines no matter the stage of their career. Through thoughtful integration of real-life scenarios and well-crafted questions for reflection, the authors align the truth of Scripture to help us grow as servants of common grace. Being on the frontlines as a Christian healthcare professional is challenging, but Sherr, Lee, and Mickle offer biblical encouragement for the weary and remind us that we are not alone in the journey. On every page, they point to the God who is our help and our hope as he guides us by his amazing grace and perfect provision to be servants of common grace."

—**Kimberly Fenstermacher**, RN, assistant dean of nursing and professor, Messiah University

"Healthcare is hard. Fortunately, we can trade our despair for hope as Christian healthcare workers. *Scripture and Scrubs* will encourage health profession students, novice healthcare workers, and seasoned professionals by reminding us not only about how we serve but also whom we serve."

—**Judy Gregg**, DNP, RN, dean of the school of nursing and health sciences, Mount Vernon Nazarene University

"There is often an expectation of those who minister on the frontlines of healthcare to be superhuman, possessing limitless knowledge and resilience. *Scriptures and Scrubs* provides inspiration and encouragement for those living their purpose as ministers of God's grace through their calling as dedicated healthcare professionals. I pray this work will be a special blessing to your spirit as it has been to mine."

—**Peter John Ramsey**, chief scientific officer and head of research and development, Haleon Healthcare

"*Scripture and Scrubs* offers a vital perspective for both students and seasoned healthcare professionals by addressing their unique challenges while integrating profound theological insights. With relatable anecdotes, theological reflections, and practical applications, this book serves as a beacon of encouragement and guidance for Christian healthcare providers, emphasizing the importance of serving as ambassadors for Christ. With its thoughtful blend of scholarship and pastoral care, it's an indispensable resource for those seeking to embody God's grace in their healthcare practice."

—**Matthew Stanford**, chief executive officer, Hope and Healing Center and Institute

"*Scripture and Scrubs* is essential reading for every Christian healthcare provider seeking to understand the 'how' and 'why' behind the difficult 'what' of their practice. Michael, Jason, and Angie provide realistic perspectives for working in healthcare while also offering vital encouragement. Reading *Scripture and Scrubs* has reinvigorated my love of nursing, and I know it will do the same for the next reader."

—**Hayden Vroegop**, BSN, CFRN, RN, NREMT, PHI Air Medical

Scripture *and* Scrubs

Scripture *and* Scrubs

A Christian Calling to Healthcare

MICHAEL E. SHERR, JASON K. LEE,

AND ANGELIA M. MICKLE

Foreword by Samuel W. "Dub" Oliver

ACADEMIC®
BRENTWOOD, TENNESSEE

Scripture and Scrubs: A Christian Calling to Healthcare

Published by B&H Academic®
Brentwood, Tennessee

ISBN: 978-1-0877-8922-4

Dewey Decimal Classification: 610.7
Subject Heading: MEDICAL PERSONNEL--CALL AND TRAINING \ MINISTRY \ VOCATION--CHRISTIANITY

The web addresses referenced in this book were live and correct at the time of the book's publication but may be subject to change.

Cover design by Lindy Kasler. Cover images by Shutterstock.

Printed in the United States of America
30 29 28 27 26 25 VP 1 2 3 4 5 6 7 8 9 10

Dedication

To the faithful servants caring for others on the front lines

CONTENTS

Acknowledgments xi
Foreword xv
Preface xix

Introduction: Thriving and Enduring through the High Calling 1

Part I:
What Are You?

1. At the Front Lines: Primary Care and the Prime Mover 11
2. God of the Bible 29
3. Servants of Common Grace 57

Part II:
What Do You Do?

4. Comfort 85
5. Forgiveness 107
6. A Greater Glory 129
7. Jars of Clay 149
8. Ambassadorship 167
9. Strategies for Thriving and Enduring 187

Name and Subject Index 201
Scripture Index 209

ACKNOWLEDGMENTS

All of us:
Thanks to our students (current and former) at Cedarville University who are answering God's call to the front lines. Our conversations with you all prompt many of this book's discussions. Thanks to the CU administration and our faculty colleagues for your support and encouragement. It is a privilege to teach at an institution that shares the vision of this book. Thanks to B&H Academic for their support of our vision of helping students and current healthcare professionals with biblical encouragement.

Michael:
I am grateful for my friends and colleagues, Angie and Jason, for working alongside me to bring this book to fruition. I appreciate the conversations over coffee and meals together as we developed a shared purpose for being a source of encouragement for Christian health professionals living out their relationships with Jesus Christ on the front lines. I am grateful to Dr. White and the rest of the administration at Cedarville University for cultivating a campus ethos elevating the importance of biblical integration in our teaching, scholarship, and service. I am grateful for the guys at the Saturday morning men's discipleship group, the patients I serve at Maranatha Family Counseling, and my church family. The love and

support from my family allowed me to spend the long hours writing. I love you, Stacey. Thank you for loving me and our family so well. Brandon (and Anna), Noah (and Grace), and Gracie (and Brett), you always fill my heart with love and joy.

Jason:

My first gratitude is for my friend and coauthor, Michael, for our year of conversations that eventually led to the idea of writing a book together. I appreciate that you pursued me for encouragement. I am grateful for my role at Cedarville University as the Director of the Center for Biblical Integration that has prompted many interdisciplinary conversations with my godly colleagues. I am grateful for my ministry role at Heritage Fellowship Church in Springfield, Ohio that helps me remember all those believers who head to the front lines every week. In all endeavors, I am grateful for the constant support of my wife, Kimberly. She and my kids and their spouses lurk behind everything that I do. Thanks, Kimberly, McKayla (and Grant), Hayden (and Taylor), Graham (and Kaite), Jackson, McKenzie, and Abbey. You all bring joy to me.

Angie:

I am sincerely grateful to my friend and colleague, Michael, who selflessly builds into my life every day, impacting both my spiritual and scholarly growth like no other. I am grateful for my role at Cedarville University as the Dean for the School of Nursing. It is a sheer privilege to serve with godly colleagues whose primary focus is being the hands and feet of Jesus, using nursing as our ministry for Christ. I am grateful for Lighthouse Baptist Church in Xenia, Ohio whose mission is to glorify God supremely, love people where they are, and carry out the great commission with passion. My church family continually reignites my passion to serve. And finally, my family, who constantly support all of my crazy endeavors. I adore my husband, Rick—I love you. Our four children—Alexis (and Ryan), Ricky (and Emily), Amanda (and Collin), and Jacob—my precious gifts. Last but not least, the eight grandchildren—being Gigi fills my heart more than they will ever know.

All of us:
To God be the glory . . . His gracious work through Christ is the reason for this book.

FOREWORD

"Come to me, all of you who are weary and burdened, and I will give you rest. Take my yoke upon you and learn from me, because I am lowly and humble in heart, and you will find rest for your souls. For my yoke is easy and my burden is light."—Matt 11:28–30

We don't want to merely survive; we want to thrive. No matter our profession, we want to thrive. That is particularly true for people in the healing professions. Their calling is to help people thrive. But we all know that being a health professional is a tremendous burden. There are so many people who are relying on you, and the risks are often very high.

How then should we live? That is a persistent question for each of us. In light of what we believe, how should we go about our work? Such is one of the challenges for Christians: how to live faithfully in the world, no matter what our calling or profession. In *Scripture and Scrubs*, Michael Sherr, Jason Lee, and Angelia Mickle guide Christian health professionals in knowing how to live out God's call faithfully and courageously in their lives.

Christian health professionals have completed years of extensive and challenging education and passed difficult licensure exams that enabled them to enter their respective professions. And yet, that is not enough to thrive. Faithfulness is needed in order to serve for the glory of God and the good of humankind. It is a sacred trust given by God to be a Christian health professional. In 1 Cor 4:2, Paul says what we all need to hear: "In this regard, it is required that managers be found faithful." *Scripture and Scrubs* will help you prove faithful to the trust given you as a Christian health professional.

You'll find in these authors people who have served on the front lines of health-care practice. Michael is a dedicated social worker, Angelia an experienced nurse, and Jason a theologian who has seen these concepts played out in the lives of those he has pastored. They bring their knowledge, experience, and love of God to this task, helping us all to live out what we believe.

Life is messy. Perhaps no group of people understand this more than healthcare professionals who see sickness and disease and brokenness (all effects of the fall) every single day of their practice. This book is designed to help faithful followers of Christ understand how the Bible shapes our thinking, motives, and desires. As we are reminded, it is one thing to realize what you are as a health professional who believes in Jesus as Lord. It is another thing to figure out how to incorporate faith into your practice. To help us see how this can happen in real life, each chapter begins with examples drawn from real-world situations that connect the reader to how this plays out in the living of our days. These scenarios cover the tremendous breadth of health care as readers find themselves in the stories, and these stories generate questions that are then thoughtfully fleshed out using Scripture as a guide.

The theology is as accessible as it is orthodox. Michael, Jason, and Angelia give a comprehensive understanding of God as revealed in the Bible, and they encourage Christian health professionals to consider the implications of these truth claims, always as a loving teacher. Their prescriptions are easy to follow, clearly connecting theology to practice, and they are biblically based. All of this, like any prescription, is designed to lead to generous health. This book presents a thorough integration of our faith in Christ with being a Christian health professional.

The authors' honesty about the vulnerability, weariness, and inherent danger of frontline service is commendable. They are straightforward about the pain experienced in the trenches. They are clear about the importance of forgiveness. And they are quick to point out help from the past—voices from the past to encourage and support you as you serve. In these pages you'll hear from Tertullian, Basil, Augustine, John Calvin, Jonathan Edwards, and Charles Haddon Spurgeon. You'll be blessed with help from above, God's Holy Spirit, God's inerrant Word, and beautiful prayers that will nourish your soul. There are questions for discussion and reflection at the end of each chapter.

If you are going to thrive long-term, embracing the high calling of a Christian health professional, you are going to need a faith rooted in God's Word. To be God's light amid the darkness and to be Christ's ambassadors to those who are hurting and who need his healing touch, you need Jesus. Christian health professionals carry an immense burden, which is why it is so important to hear Jesus say, "My yoke is easy and my burden is light," and to travel this road with him.

Early Christians valued the use of medicine for the healing of the human body. Those same early Christians recognized that it was a grace of God to give medical knowledge to humans and for the applications of medicine to bring about the desired healing. In our own day we are told to "trust the science," basically, that we should worship science. *Scripture and Scrubs* offers something better: trust the God who created the earth and everything in it. In an age when so many are telling us that our faith in Christ must be kept private, Michael, Jason, and Angelia remind us that living for Christ in the health-care professions is not only possible, but is the only way to faithfully follow our Savior.

Among the press of insurance billables, governmental regulations, organizational approvals, constantly adapting practice, and myriad needs of patients, *Scripture and Scrubs* leads the way for all who follow Christ to be ambassadors for Christ in the health-care arena.

In your hands, you are holding a resource where you will want to write notes about your own experiences in the margins, and one that you will return to again and again as you seek to become the Christian health professional God intends you to become. If your divine purpose is to serve God as his ambassadors of common grace, then the pages ahead will guide the way.

May God be glorified,
Samuel W. "Dub" Oliver, president, Union University

PREFACE

Have you ever asked yourself in the middle of a shift, *Why God? Why? What am I doing here?* I (Michael) remember working in the emergency room one evening when I got called to do a psych consultation for a sixteen-year-old girl who had just had her stomach pumped. She tried killing herself by taking over a hundred Tylenol. As I talked with her, she eventually described being the victim of years of sexual assault from her stepfather. She had just found out she was pregnant with his child. She didn't know what else to do. *Why God?*

A few years later, working as a children's hospice social worker, I arrived at the home of an eight-year-old patient who had just died from leukemia. The room was full of cigarette smoke, the five-year-old sister hugging my leg crying, and the parents sitting on the couch barely functional as they were both inebriated from too much alcohol. *How am I supposed to help these people? Why does God have me here?*

If you ever wondered or thought about how your faith, how your relationship with God should influence your practice, this book is for you. If you believe in God and take his Word seriously and your practice seriously, this book is for you. If you picked up this book and do not believe in God, maybe it is not a coincidence. We invite you to continue reading so you will understand what should be unique about Christians serving the Lord as health-care professionals.

Lord, I Just Want to Help People

I (Michael) was twenty-three when I confessed my sins, repented, and accepted Jesus Christ as Lord and Savior. Raised in a Jewish conservative home, I recognized and believed in Jesus as the Messiah after finally picking up his inerrant Word and praying to God to teach me what he wanted me to know, and him allowing me to see that Jesus is the whole point of the Bible, from the Tanakh to Revelation.

God gave me an appetite for spending time in Scripture. Since accepting Jesus as Lord, I have spent every single day in his Word. Reading God's Word is the first thing I do when I wake up and the last thing I do before going to bed. All these years later, I still find that my heart leaps for joy and anticipation when I spend time with God in prayer and in his Word. Early on, though I considered pursuing a seminary degree, deep down I just did not feel called to become a pastor. I found myself in constant prayer saying, "Lord, I just want to help people." The desire to help people struggling with physical, emotional, social, and spiritual hurt led me to a career in social work. Now as a seasoned Christian health professional and scholar, I have spent my adult life contemplating two overlapping questions: What is my purpose as a Christian health-care professional (CHP)? Does God's Word provide tangible guidance for my practice?

I know students wrestle with similar questions. I suppose most professionals wonder how their faith influences their practice. If they don't, it likely means they are coping with the demands of health-care practice by compartmentalizing their lives at church from their lives at work. I asked my friends—a theologian and a nurse educator, both colleagues at Cedarville—to help me articulate a "real-life" Christian perspective on health care. It is our intention to help you grasp how important it is for Christians to serve in health care and to inspire you to see your role through God's eternal purpose as revealed in Scripture.

Friend, Theologian, and Biblical Integration Partner

Years ago, my wife and I (Jason) were at the Aberdeen Royal Infirmary complex on a blustery day in Scotland. Our visit was not expected—my wife was suffering another miscarriage. Like on other occasions, the medical team was excellent and professional, and my wife's physical needs were met. But we were lonely. We were thousands of miles from family, and this renewed grief caused some deeper anxieties about childlessness and God's care for us. Morag, a member of the hospital team, knew I was a pastor in nearby Stonehaven. She came by to visit us in our hospital room, and as a Christian in a health-care environment, she was a godsend. She stayed only briefly but comforted our hearts with truthful words that I cannot remember in detail. Morag was an ambassador of Christ that day.

I grew up in America on the Gulf Coast in a Christian home. I came to faith in Christ relatively early in life and attended university to train as a pastor. Years later, I ended up in Scotland as a PhD student and a pastor. Many have discipled me in formal and informal settings. Additionally, I have been able to disciple people from all kinds of helping professions. My work as a professor and a pastor has been "behind-the-scenes" training for believers who are engaging professional roles of holistic care for people.

As a theologian, my research interests are in the doctrine of Scripture and the doctrine of the church. Even my academic work is done with a view toward helping churches and individual believers understand and live by their faith. I do not want to be "the kind of doctor that doesn't really help people" (as one of my children once said). I wrestle with questions like, How does the Bible shape our thinking, motives, and desires? And can I contribute to a "real-life" Christian perspective on health-care fields? As a pastor, can I show the relevance of our faith, our relationship with Jesus

Christ, and our biblical worldview to the lives of the health-care professionals in the church?

Not long ago, I accepted a role at Cedarville University where I am a theological dialogue partner with my colleagues in a variety of professional fields. As fellow disciples, Michael and I have enjoyed many hours of coffee conversations on how we can help students, professors, and current CHPs labor on the front lines of everyday life with a biblical perspective on their roles as servants of grace. This book is a pastoral effort to provide specific encouragement to Christian health-care practitioners.

Friend, Nurse Educator, and Biblical Integration Partner

I (Angie) have wanted to be a nurse since I was five years old. A strong desire to help others was embedded deep in my soul—clearly before I had any idea what being a nurse really meant, which can only point to one thing: nursing was truly the calling God had for my life. But why?

Unlike most of my colleagues, I was not raised in a Christian home. I learned about Jesus by being a "bus ministry" kid. I still thank God daily for loving parents who were willing to send me to church every Sunday so they could enjoy "free babysitting" and have some alone time. I declared myself a sinner and accepted Christ as my personal Savior at church camp when I was about seven years old. My love for Jesus and Sunday school stories guided my childhood years and helped inform mostly good decision-making as a teenager. I spent many nights singing myself to sleep to the beautiful and convicting words of "Amazing Grace." Life was far from perfect in a non-Christian home, and I continuously would ask God, *Why?*

My personal relationship with Jesus Christ strengthened two weeks after high school graduation when I left the comforts of home and started military basic training. Growing in my Christian walk has been a journey, far from easy because life is messy; but my burning desire of being a genuine beacon of light to everyone I meet drives me daily.

As I reflect on my life of fifty-five years, I feel like I have garnered over 200 years of life experience. Thirty-three of those years I have been living my childhood dream, but why? My professional nursing career spans emergency, flight, home health, family practice, and psyche mental health experiences; this nursing journey has culminated in my current role as nurse educator. Every day I love my job and cannot believe I get paid to be a nurse.

Through all my personal and professional transformations, a few things have remained constant: I love being a nurse now more than ever; my love for King Jesus grows deeper every day; I am first and foremost a child of God. I am excited about penning my stories, aspiring to help other health-care professionals make sense of their "why". My prayer is to help them reignite their professional passion, recognize their privilege of caring for others, and love their daily practice situations, knowing they can do so through the strength they receive from Jesus. Everyone is important in their health-care role. Many are responding to a calling God has placed on them. Nothing happens by chance—his mercies are new every day, and he has already given us everything we need.

Introduction:

Thriving and Enduring through the High Calling

Representing God at the front lines is an amazing way to live for Jesus Christ. We spend our lives ready in love to bear all things, believe in all things, hope in all things, and endure all things (1 Cor 13:7). But it is dangerous and wearisome on the front lines. Health professionals have some of the highest rates of vicarious trauma, burnout, drug and alcohol addiction, and suicidal ideation. Answering the vocational call to serve as CHPs is too much to endure only through deep breathing exercises or self-help strategies. A lukewarm faith, a childlike zeal with minimal grasp of the gospel, or a moral sense of obligation to do the right thing will simply not be enough amid the unvarnished havoc of patient scenarios that seem to outdo one another in the level of depravity thought possible. If you are going to thrive long-term embracing the high calling of a CHP, you are going to need rock-solid faith rooted in God's Word. Though making time for Scripture should be a priority for every believer, the challenges for health-care professionals make it indisputable. You want to endure and serve Christ well in health care? You must take Scripture as seriously as you take health-care practice.

Answering the call to be a CHP can be such a rewarding way for serving God to further his kingdom. We want to help you thrive by grasping your calling from within the context of God's Word. To do so, we organize the book into two sections so that you are clear about your role on the front line and can fulfill your role effectively. We first present a theologically grounded purpose for CHPs so that you can articulate exactly what you are with clarity. We then present five spiritual competencies, so you know exactly what you do as an effective CHP. The spiritual competencies are biblically grounded principles, practices, beliefs, and virtues that stem from our relationship with God. It is our relationship with Jesus Christ that gives us our purpose as CHPs. It is also our relationship with Jesus Christ that cultivates the spiritual competencies necessary to fulfill our purpose effectively. The two sections should reinforce what you are and what you do as a CHP. Taking time to answer the few reflection/discussion questions at the end of each chapter will help reinforce what you need to get the most out of this book. Let us provide a brief summary of the chapters ahead.

In chapter 2 we describe the God of the Bible. We believe God reveals in his Word how CHPs should approach their work as stewards of God's grace. We also believe his Word provides direction for thriving at the front lines. However, random verses taken out of context will not provide the firm foundation needed for the CHP. Scripture is the inspired revelation of God in texts. These texts as God's Word are truthful and authoritative as God's guidance to his people. The sufficiency of the Bible to address our lives and professional practices is confirmed as we recognize his divine guidance of human authors. These inspired texts are to be read as part of a coherent whole ("the Bible," "the Scriptures," or "the biblical canon"). In these biblical books, down to individual passages, God reveals himself and his revealed plan to accomplish the salvation of men and women. Every word, every verse, every chapter, and every book of the Bible must be understood within the context of the whole of Scripture.

Chapter 3 introduces God's purpose for CHPs within the context of his revealed plan. CHPs are at the front lines as *servants of common grace.* "Common grace" is a term that describes the goodness and kindness of God to all humanity. For Christians who take Scripture seriously, serving in health care is both a professional and spiritual journey. Part of that journey is navigating the constant internal struggle between playing things safe by compartmentalizing professional practice from spiritual life or living one complete integrated life. The temptation to set aside your beliefs as you enter the hospital for another shift will always be there. Embracing God's purpose as a servant of common grace can help you overcome that temptation. As a servant of common grace, you work every shift as God's representative where you help temporarily restrain and mitigate the damaging consequences of sin and enable people to experience the goodness of his creation. Most importantly, by caring for their physical and mental well-being, you help afford people time to hear (in some instances from you) the gospel so that they might confess and repent of their sins and receive Jesus Christ as Lord and Savior. This hope will help sustain them as they come to grips with their mortality.

We then transition to the spiritual competencies for serving as servants of common grace. Within the context of the biblical narrative, we take a closer look at Paul's second epistle to the Corinthians. In what may be Paul's most pastoral letter, he points to several theological themes whereby believers can incorporate their faith and love for Jesus Christ into their practice. We consider these themes as the spiritual competencies CHPs need to serve patients effectively on the front lines.

Comfort is the first spiritual competency. Chapter 4 explores the depth of what Paul means by comfort. As servants of common grace, we support people when they are in trouble. We help sustain them when they are suffering. We reassure them in the midst of their distress. We share abundantly when they experience relief. We have received comfort from God and are thereby qualified to share that comfort with others.

Chapter 5 calls attention to forgiveness as the second spiritual competency. CHPs, perhaps more often than any other professionals, work with patients who are confronted with the consequences of sin. When we see patients in need of care from physical ailments, mental ailments, or poor decisions and judgments that caused harm, we are confronted by our own history of sin. At one point or another, we have all been grieved and have been the cause of grief for others. A biblically informed posture of forgiveness is how God wants us to thrive amid that grief. God wants us to exercise forgiveness in our professional and personal lives so we can be as effective as possible with patients and colleagues.

For servants of common grace, forgiveness is multilayered. You forgive to free yourself of excessive sorrow. You forgive to reaffirm your love for yourself as God's child, for your patients, and for your colleagues. You forgive to remain obedient to God who sends you out to be his servant of common grace. You forgive because it is rooted in Christ's forgiveness, which transcends grief with radical love and radical mercy. You forgive knowing that Satan is ready for any opportunity to try to outwit you, steal your joy, and make you question your relationship with God and your purpose on the front lines.

Another joy of serving as CHPs is the opportunity to point patients toward a greater glory—the third spiritual competency. In chapter 6 we contrast our work with the flesh as health-care providers and our work through the Holy Spirit as followers of Jesus Christ. CHPs know that the care we provide patients only offers a foretaste of the glory of God. The restoration we provide to patients is fragile and temporary. Regardless of how much training, skill, or experience we have, we will have patients seeking care where we are powerless to help. There will always be routine procedures that do not go as planned and patients who have unexpected reactions to medications. Even when patients fully recover from illnesses or heal from injuries, the "newness" of their lives will eventually fade. So, as important as it is to treat patients with sound and effective practices, servants of common grace are always there to point patients toward permanent glory—eternal life through confession, repentance, and belief in the life, death, resurrection, and ascension of Jesus Christ our Lord and Savior.

Permanent glory changes things for CHPs. Temporal well-being, though of some value, is just not as important when living within the assurance of the unbreakable relationship we have with Jesus. God can now use whatever depths of personal and professional hardships endured in our lives to make us even more effective as servants of common grace. Through the work of the Holy Spirit, we become lights in the thick of darkness. In other words, God transforms us into "jars of clay," the fourth spiritual competence (see 2 Cor 4:7). Chapter 7 examines what happens when trials and suffering become part of our testimony as CHPs. As we are afflicted but not crushed, perplexed but not in despair, and persecuted but not forsaken, we develop the capacity for strategic vulnerability with patients. Whatever patients suffer, however hurt or weak they feel, we can engage them in their sense of powerlessness or helplessness. We can engage with patients because we know the depths of our own brokenness. More importantly, we know where we (and they) can find joy amid the pain—in grace alone, though faith alone, in Christ alone.

The joy of having a personal relationship with the Savior of the world transforms everything we do in health care. It even transforms who we really are when we step before our patients and colleagues as CHPs. Nothing we do in our work remains mundane. Every lab test we run, every patient interaction, every X-ray, every conversation with friends seeking help for health care, mental health, or substance abuse issues, and every messy devastating situation we encounter on the front lines, we step in as stewards of God's grace and as God's representatives for the Son, Jesus Christ. In other words, we are his ambassadors.

Chapter 8 examines ambassadorship as the last spiritual competency. We view ambassadorship as the meta-competency. It is the culmination of what happens as CHPs serve effectively as servants of common grace. As the Holy Spirit refines you for providing patients comfort, forgiveness, pointing to permanent glory, and serving as jars of clay, he does so for a reason. God can make himself known to patients and colleagues through you. Your care will display his love for his creatures; with your words you can explain the greatest demonstration of his love, Christ's death for us (Rom 5:8).

You have two purposes as his ambassador. On one hand, you are there to love and care for people so they may encounter Jesus Christ as God the Son. On the other hand, you provide testimony to God's common grace so that all are without an excuse (Rom 1:19–20). It is God who fulfills both purposes. There is no pressure to discern which role we are fulfilling. We are free to engage in professional health-care practice knowing both will happen, being prepared to give the reason for our joy, even amid suffering, full of grace and seasoned with salt.

We finish the book by offering strategies for thriving and enduring as servants of common grace. Although there is an element of gaining practical experience as CHPs, we don't necessarily work on developing our spiritual competencies the way we do our professional expertise. It has more to do with the posture of our hearts and our minds. As we worship and obey the Lord with a heartfelt response and desire to submit to and follow after Jesus Christ, he will undoubtedly develop the spiritual competences. In chapter 9 we describe seven strategies for faithful worship for CHPs wanting to be intentional about growing in their relationship with the Lord. The strategies are really for any Christian wanting to grow in their relationship with God. We urge CHPs, however, to consider these as essential for being faithful servants on the front lines. The seven described briefly here are:

1. Continuous Training—Must be faithful in seeking continuous training in areas of professional practice *AND* learning more and more about God's Word.
2. Prayer—Must develop a robust prayer life.
3. Practice or Embrace Sabbath Rest—Learning to abide in him, instead of striving and over-functioning which can lead to burnout.

4. Perspective on the Harvest and the Work—God saves. He does not need us. Instead, he allows us to participate in the ministry, in the harvest.
5. Find Brother-in-Christ or Sister-in-Christ Relationships—Need a discipleship relationship with someone who "gets it" who can help you learn from experiences through the lens of Scripture.
6. Christian Fellowship—Healthy outlet for rest and respite with other Christian brothers and sisters to reenergize you for the ministry at hand.
7. Consider Missions—Local and global missions can bring new energy and an eternal perspective to reinvigorate the work/ministry right before you.

PART I

What Are You?

In one way or another, every Christian must determine their identity. You may be a mom, a dad, a brother, a sister, or a friend. You may be a musician, an athlete, a leader, or a follower. You may be a nurse, a doctor, a psychologist, a social worker, a pharmacist, or a radiologist. I (Jason) am a theologian professionally. I have an advanced degree in theology. I teach theology to undergraduate, graduate, and doctoral students. I am a theologian at my church where I preach and teach as a pastor. However, I am also a theologian on our back porch with my wife as we talk through a recent podcast that she has listened to. I am a theologian with my kids as we ride down the road and discuss their "Why does God . . ." questions. Whether you know it or not, as a Christian you are also a theologian. You are a theologian because, as someone who believes that Jesus is Lord, you must figure out where being a follower of Jesus fits in your life. The answer of course is a paradox as it is simple and comprehensive, unchanging and transformational. Jesus Christ deserves to be first in your life. He wants your relationship with him to define your identity. He even wants to be the reason you work in health care *and* he wants your health-care practice to be an ongoing form of worship.

We (Michael and Angie) know this paradox well. On the one hand, it seems so obvious. Put Christ first, got it. Practice as worship, well . . . sure, okay. On the other hand, what exactly does that mean for us? Is Michael a Christian social worker, a Christian in social work, or a Christian and a social worker? Does he practice social work differently from social workers who are not Christians? Is Angie a Christian nurse, a nurse who happens to be a Christian, or a nurse and a Christian? Does she practice differently from nurses who are not Christians? What about you? What are you?

You are a Christian health professional. In fact, every Christian working in health care is a Christian health professional. We use part one of the book to highlight the unique distinctive that we all share. Regardless of actual job title, we uncover our purpose from within the context of all Scripture, and we claim our roles as *servants of common grace*.

Chapter 1

At the Front Lines: Primary Care and the Prime Mover

For although we live in the flesh, we do not wage war according to the flesh, since the weapons of our warfare are not of the flesh, but are powerful through God . . . —2 Cor 10:3–4a

Can you tell if the health-care professionals described below are Christians? Does it matter? Let us frame the question a bit differently: Should there be anything distinctive about Christians serving in the kinds of situations described below?

Lisa Faye—Family Nurse Practitioner

Lisa works at a rural health family practice clinic. Twenty years of nursing experience culminated in this advanced practice role, which she has thoroughly enjoyed these past four years. Her patient panel has grown exponentially, and she absolutely loves the variety of patient scenarios seen in a single day. Recently, the office has been running with less support staff. In fact, ever since opening back up after months of telehealth due to COVID, the office has resumed operating with less than half of the previous administrative and support staff.

Today, like most days, Lisa's schedule is completely full, and she notes that a new patient has just been added to her schedule, causing a "double booked" time slot right before lunch. This causes Lisa to groan, knowing her lunch "break" has just been cut in half. In her mind, she secretly desires a no-show to help lighten the load.

Lisa's morning unfolds and she is only running about ten minutes behind when she goes in to meet a sweet fourteen-year-old new patient named Courtney. Courtney's chief complaint is persistent nausea which began about three weeks earlier. Lisa collects the new patient's history while working to establish a rapport. The physical exam is unremarkable and confirms that this healthy teenage volleyball player is a picture of health who should be able to compete without difficulties. While interacting with Courtney, Lisa recognizes that the communication between Courtney and her mom is strained and that Courtney seems very timid. Courtney's mom is also a nurse; she and Lisa used to work together at the local hospital.

Lisa completes a brief workup and quickly determines Courtney's urine pregnancy test is positive. Lisa's hunger and shortened lunch hour are now minimized in her mind as she contemplates how best to deliver the news of an unplanned pregnancy to Courtney and her mother.

Keith Salentiny—Geriatric Pharmacist

Keith Salentiny is a geriatric pharmacist at a level-four assisted living facility. He works mostly with older patients who often need 24-hour continuous assistance. They often need help walking, bathing, eating, and getting out of their beds. The patients receive care from an entire multidisciplinary team of health-care professionals. Doctors, nurses, dieticians, physical therapists, speech therapists, recreation therapists, certified nursing assistants, and social workers work together to ensure the highest quality of life possible as patients cope with a host of ailments that emerge as people get older. The patients often take a lot of different medications, making Keith a vital member of the team.

A typical shift for Keith involves two primary responsibilities—chart reviews and patient/family consultations. Though his tasks are important, his work can often feel redundant and tedious. For instance, because patients are being cared for by so many different health professionals, his shifts always begin with reviewing the charts of every patient. For patients in a level-four facility, medication management is a continuous, delicate balance of treating primary care issues, treating complications brought upon by the medications, and treating ancillary issues such as pain and incontinence. Keith must carefully review all new medications or changes in medications to make sure they will not interfere with the patients' overall care. He is also tasked with assessing and minimizing the costs of the medication regimens for the facility and the patients. He then needs to work with members of the multidisciplinary team to make adjustments in dosage or recommend changes. Afterward, he spends the remainder of each day consulting with patients and family members to advise them of the rationale for the changes made.

Once every quarter, Keith participates in a quality assessment and assurance meeting. The meeting focuses on maintaining performance standards to ensure adherence to state and local laws and regulations, and to implement any needed corrective actions. He then incorporates the corrective actions into his regular patient chart reviews.

Judy Aikens—Mammography Technologist

Judy has been performing mammograms at the local county hospital for nearly twenty years. Judy's career in radiology consisted of taking X-rays for the first few years after becoming a radiology technician. When Judy was twenty-three years old, her mom was diagnosed with breast cancer. As a result of her mom's journey, she became passionate about specializing in the field of mammography. Judy went back to school to become a licensed, board-certified mammographer.

Judy spends all her time providing screening to women (and men) when they are feeling their most vulnerable. Her goal is to make each patient feel comfortable and respected while obtaining pictures of breast tissue that can be difficult to obtain because every patient's habitus is different.

This morning the radiology registration clerk called off work because of an ill child. Judy works in a skeleton-staffed department and there was no one to cover. Judy's schedule was full and now she needs to check patients in and get their paperwork completed before obtaining their mammograms. The morning went better than she expected, and lunch was a welcomed break. Unfortunately, the afternoon was a different story. Her second patient, sixty-five-year-old Rita, had not had a screening mammogram done since she was forty. Judy was alarmed to read about this lapse in care when reviewing the patient intake information.

Rita was vibrant, kind, and full of life. Judy found her to be cooperative while obtaining the pictures, and the women conversed like they had known each other for years. After images of the right breast were completed, Judy moved to the left breast and quickly obtained the scout view. Much to her surprise, she noticed a huge mass in the left breast at the six o'clock position. Judy's mind was immediately flooded with memories of her mom's battle with breast cancer and wondered how she was going to be able to complete this mammogram, fully aware of how this discovery was going to play out.

Pam Carson—Social Worker

Pam Carson arrived at the hospital for her shift at 7:00 a.m. as usual. She made her way to the staff lounge, then met with the attending physician and nurse supervisor so they could review needs on the unit. As the medical social worker assigned to the thirty-bed acute rehabilitation unit, Pam spends most of her time assessing new patients as they are admitted to the unit, providing emotional support or counseling to patients and families, completing comprehensive social histories, and developing discharge plans when patients are ready to transition to sub-acute care or outpatient providers. She is on the move from the time her shift begins until she leaves at 4:00 in the afternoon.

Today, Pam needs to complete discharge plans for two patients ready to move to outpatient care. The first patient was referred to recover from surgery. The patient was airlifted to the hospital after suffering a skiing accident. The severity of the injuries to her lower extremities resulted in below-knee amputation of both legs. After three weeks of intensive care involving pain management, physical therapy, and crisis intervention counseling for her and her family, the patient is well enough to return home. The second patient was admitted to the unit after suffering an ischemic stroke. The stroke caused complete visual loss and paralysis of her left side. The physician prescribed the patient an anticoagulant and an ACE inhibitor. After five days on the unit, the patient is ready to return home. Pam needs to develop individualized plans for both patients. She needs to interview both patients and their families, engage with their insurance companies, and establish referrals for follow-up care that will involve various medical appointments, pain management, occupational therapy, and transportation services. She needs to have both patients out of the unit within twenty-four hours.

Tanya Joyner-Williams—Emergency Physician

Tanya transitioned from being an Air Force physician a few years ago. She retired as a lieutenant colonel and moved back to her hometown. Following a few months of getting settled, she accepted a position in the emergency medicine unit at the nearby Veterans Administration (VA) medical center. She works twelve-hour shifts seeing patients triaged from walk-in levels of care to critical condition. Depending on her initial examination of patients, she links them to backup services in surgery, psychiatry, and other medical subspecialties. She also must initiate in-patient admission procedures when she determines that extended hospital care is needed. When Tanya is not working at the VA medical center, she volunteers one day a month to see patients for free at a local rescue mission. The past three summers, she also traveled to Kyampisi, Uganda, as part of a missions team from her church serving at a children's center that rescues and rehabilitates children saved from human trafficking.

Tanya looks forward to her mission work each summer. She finds that the time she spends at the children's center revitalizes her love of medicine. It confirms her dependence on God. It also reminds her of his love for the poor and the orphaned. She is always struck by the endless joy she experiences from the children and the staff, even during exceedingly difficult living conditions. Along with two other members from her church, Tanya lugged all the donated and purchased supplies from her church to create a makeshift clinic at the center—the only time the children will have access to adequate medical care. She will spend most of the next eleven days seeing patients from sunrise to sunset. She knows that once word gets out that medical care is available, there will be people from the nearby village lined up to see her for all medical conditions.

Are They Christians? Does It Matter?

Well, can you tell if Lisa Faye, Kevin Salentiny, Judy Aikens, or Pam Carson are Christians? What about Tanya Joyner-Williams? Based on Tanya's case vignette, you might presume she is—based on knowing she attends a church and has engaged in mission work the past few years. But pause for a minute and reread her case again. Focus and think deeper about her actual practices and behaviors as a physician. Couldn't any physician, regardless of religious beliefs, carry out the same types of medical care? Does Tanya's relationship with Jesus Christ as Lord and Savior change the dynamics of her work at all? What about the others? If we stated at the beginning that all the case vignettes involved Christians serving in a variety of health-care professions, should it change what they do or how they do it? We believe it should. All the case vignettes were, in fact, about Christians working in health-care professions. We believe there *is* something different that separates them from their colleagues. We believe what makes them unique *should* influence their practice.

It is important for Christians to serve in health care. When men and women with vibrant relationships with Jesus Christ work in health care, it transforms their practice. For the Christian, God's Word provides tangible guidance for transforming their lives and therefore transforming their practices in health care as well as other areas of life. Our intent here is to help Christians serving in health care unlock the tangible guidance provided in Scripture for transforming their lives and their practice. But first, let us describe what we mean by Christian health professionals.

Christian Health Professionals

So what do we mean by Christian health professionals (CHP)? We use the term CHP to describe Christian men and women who work in a broad range of health-care settings, performing a diverse array of functions and tasks. Physicians, nurses, psychologists, social workers, and pharmacists are all CHPs. But so are phlebotomists, certified nursing assistants, physical therapists, occupational therapists, athletic trainers, nutritionists, physician assistants, and others. It may seem as if Lisa Faye, Kevin Salentiny, Judy Aikens, Pam Carson, and Tanya Joyner-Williams serve in distinct roles and do different things. We believe, however, that they share characteristics that unify them with all other CHPs. These characteristics contribute to why health-care practice is so demanding and challenging. They are also what makes health-care practice such a unique form of ministry. Christians in health care are called to action by God, the prime mover, to serve him on the front lines, to remind people of their mortality, and to live out professional codes of ethics.

Prime Mover

Originally, God created humans in his image, including his gift of life. He blessed their life with purpose (priestly dominion and production) and with harmonious relationships with their Creator and their fellow creatures. Human life was to begin with natural birth ("be fruitful and multiply" in Gen 1:28) and would continue perpetually because the humans had access to the wondrous tree of life (Gen 2:9) as God's gift. This perfect design would not last long because of human sin and would need redemption if the created world, and humans specifically, were to be rescued. More on that part of the story in chapter 2.

In the thirteenth century, the theologian St. Thomas Aquinas wrote of "Five Ways" to defend the existence of God. Drawing on the ideas of the Greek philosopher Aristotle, Aquinas explained that the existence of the material world demanded a "first cause" or the "prime mover." For Aquinas, the Bible described the work of God the Creator in such a way that the God of the Bible fills the role of the prime mover.[1] By implication, remaining aspects of order in a now chaotic world point to the steadying hand of a Creator. CHPs are often the access people have to the orderliness of God's design even as they grapple with the chaos of our fallen condition. Stated differently, CHPs provide primary care as they represent the prime mover.

Serve on the Front Lines

There is a difference between serving in the background and serving at the front lines. When children play board games that require any strategy, they learn to recognize the roles of pieces very quickly. For instance, players often use the pieces at the front in checkers to engage the opponent's pieces way before the pieces on the backline ever get moved. In the same way, the

[1] Alister E. McGrath, *Historical Theology: An Introduction to the History of Christian Thought* (Malden, MA: Blackwell, 1998), 130–33.

pawns in chess serve at the front line where they are the first line of defense for the king. Though weak on their own, when deployed effectively by a skillful player, they create the conditions on the board that make checkmate possible. When pawns reach the last row on an opponent's side of the board, they are transformed into another piece, typically the queen—the most powerful piece on the board. This transformation usually makes checkmate a forgone conclusion.

In 1 Samuel 16–17, God transformed David. At the beginning of this story, David was a young and insignificant servant in King Saul's nation (and the least of his own brothers). When David arrived at King Saul's encampment with the provisions at the battle line, he heard Goliath challenge the soldiers of Israel to send forth one warrior in a winner-takes-all fight to the death. His challenge left all the soldiers of Israel afraid, and they all fled. The soldiers were supposed to be serving on the front lines, but they retreated to the rear. David, full of faith in the Lord, transformed in steps from what others perceived to be a weak, insignificant young man, to God's servant at the front line in a battle of life and death. He represented God in everything that truly mattered to God.

CHPs, too, represent God on the front lines when it really matters. In every health profession, Christians find themselves engaging people in their greatest time of need. CHPs often interact with patients who are hurting or feeling ill. It was the feeling of nausea that brought Courtney in to see Lisa Faye. Pam Carson was working with patients who will need long-term help coping with physical and psychological pain. Their discharge from the acute rehabilitation facility is likely only the beginning of their healing and suffering. Tanya Joyner-Williams never knows what will bring patients to see her at the VA. She does know that every patient she encounters has experienced enough of a disruption in their life to seek care in the emergency room.

People are physically and emotionally the most vulnerable at the front lines. CHPs ask patients to trust them as they perform physical examinations that can be invasive and uncomfortable. Patients often talk with

CHPs about their most personal and private matters. Annual physicals can become a time of reflection for patients as physicians, nurse practitioners, or physician assistants ask them about their diets, stress levels, and physical or emotional discomforts. Abuses, regrets, bad decisions, or the consequences of bad decisions are shared between patients and CHPs. During extended rehabilitation from injuries, patients rely on physical therapists or athletic trainers to help process the trauma that caused their injuries, their frustrations with the slow, grinding pace of recovery, and their fears of being unable to return to "normal" functioning. Sometimes CHPs must help patients cope with a new "normal" level of functioning that limits what they can do from this point forward. Sometimes, CHPs must tell patients they are not going to recover, and that they are dying. In all situations, CHPs always remind patients of their mortality.

Remind People of their Mortality

If you are like us (Michael and Angie), you went into your health profession seeking to help people. You endured (or are enduring) many years of schooling, the long shifts at work, and the endless studying with the expectation of helping patients prevent injury, heal, and recover. And, while you may experience the blessing of being part of healing patients, your very presence is evidence to them of God's curse to Adam and Eve in the garden of Eden. Pause right now. Take time to reflect on God's declaration in Gen 3:16–19:

> He said to the woman: "I will intensify your labor pains; you will bear children with painful effort. Your desire will be for your husband, yet he will rule over you." And he said to the man, "Because you listened to your wife and ate from the tree about which I commanded you, 'Do not eat from it': The ground is cursed because of you. You will eat from it by means of painful labor all the days of your life. It will produce thorns and thistles for you, and you will eat the plants of the field. You will eat bread by the sweat of your

brow until you return to the ground, since you were taken from it.
For you are dust, and you will return to dust."

Notice the consequences of Adam and Eve's disobedience: a broken world ("The ground is cursed because of you"). From that point forth, human lives would be marked by experiencing sorrow, pain, unhealthy desires, discomfort, exhaustion, sweat, injuries, and death. CHPs know this from their training. As much as we see evidence of divine creation in the intricate and unique design of how human bodies develop and function, we also learn all the ways the human body can be injured, become ill, and eventually die.

Experiencing physical and psychological pain is now inevitable. Our bodies get injured. We all know the discomfort that comes with grieving, feeling sorrow, or enduring hardships and disappointments. We see patients when they are run-down from work, weakened when they lack adequate food, and anxious, depressed, and even suicidal when they get overwhelmed by the toils of life. Wellness checks and preventative care are times for CHPs to screen patients for things they may experience at some point in their lives. Acute care is a time for CHPs to treat patients to bring them temporary healing and stave off an early death. Palliative care is a time for CHPs to provide patients comfort and quality-of-life care when they are terminally ill. From pediatrics to geriatrics, CHPs engage patients in matters of life and death.

Here is the reality. Doctors, nurses, social workers, etc., were not needed before Genesis 3. Because of the fall, all CHPs serve two theological and practical purposes. Both of these purposes are extensions of the grace of God. First, CHPs help men and women cope with the fallout of our disobedience and rebellion. Pain and suffering were introduced to the human experience due to human sin, and yet CHPs can provide temporary relief from some aspects of this pain and suffering. Second, CHPs serve as a constant reminder that eventually the breath of life (Gen 2:7) will leave our flesh and we will return to the ground as dust. A bad medical diagnosis delivered by a caring physician blends divine grace and human mortality. God's original design focused on the life God gave, not the death humans earned.

Oaths and Professional Codes of Ethics

Representing God (the prime mover) in health care occurs within the context of various professional commitments. CHPs can never practice health care completely independent from rules and regulations. They often work within the constraints of the policies and procedures of government boards, local hospitals, clinics, and/or agencies. Ahead of all the other outside expectations, CHPs are guided by their professional organizations. Professional organizations define the parameters for entering different CHPs. They also establish standards for ethical practice. While examining the codes from various disciplines is beyond the scope of this book, one similarity exists near the front of all of the documents that unifies CHPs. Take a look at the statements from a few of the different codes of ethics. Can you identify the common theme?

- American Nurses Association—The nurse practices with compassion and respect for the inherent dignity, worth, and unique attributes of every person.
- American Medical Association—A physician shall be dedicated to providing competent medical care, with compassion and respect for human dignity and rights.
- National Association of Social Workers—Social workers' primary responsibility is to promote the well-being of clients.
- American Pharmacists Association—A pharmacist promotes the good of every patient in a caring, compassionate, and confidential manner.
- American Physical Therapy Association—Physical therapists shall be trustworthy and compassionate in addressing the rights and needs of patients and clients.
- American Society of Radiologic Technologists—The radiologic technologist delivers patient care and service unrestricted by concerns of personal attributes of the nature of the disease or illness,

and without discrimination on the basis of sex, race, creed, religion, or socioeconomic status.

- National Athletic Trainers' Association—In the role of an athletic trainer, members shall practice with compassion, respecting the rights, well-being, and dignity of others.
- American Academy of Physician Assistants—Physician assistants hold as their primary responsibility the health, safety, welfare, and dignity of all human beings.

All CHPs take an oath to serve *every* person in need of help. We do not have the luxury of choosing whom we serve. Race, ethnicity, religious beliefs, nationalities, social class, sexual orientation, homelife, or any other variable has no bearing. Every patient can expect to receive competent, ethical care. CHPs take an oath to care for Christian patients and non-believers. We help genuinely nice people and verifiable scoundrels. We serve the victims and the offenders. We treat the abusers and the abused. We help naive rambunctious teenagers and prisoners incarcerated for the most heinous of crimes. If you can imagine the most bizarre and difficult patients doing the most destructive and disturbing things, CHPs will be there ready to engage, assess, and intervene as effectively as possible again and again and again. We will be there serving God at the front lines, helping people cope with disobedience and rebellion, and reminding them of their mortality.

Our Confidence in God's Help

We suspect that reading this far may bring a mix of emotions and thoughts. Grasping our high calling as CHPs took shape through years of taking God's Word seriously as we continued fulfilling our oaths to help patients and equip future CHPs to help patients. We get it, Christian health-care practice can feel dangerous, overwhelming, joyful, and meaningful—all at the same time! When I (Jason) try to encourage my son and daughter-in-law as young CHPs, I realize how incredibly difficult, and sometimes lonely, their service to others can be. Serving God obediently on the front lines comes with the highest of highs and the lowest of lows.

This book is shaped by our commitment to encourage you as a CHP. Whether you are a student or an experienced professional, our objective is the same. We want to help you grow in your relationship with the Good Shepherd and run with endurance the race he set before you. Embracing your calling as a servant of common grace and allowing God to transform you through the spiritual competencies will help you joyfully endure to the end. We are confident God will help you because our confidence comes from our faith in the Son, revealed to us within the context of the whole Bible, his complete and perfect Word.

You Are Not Alone—Help from the Past

From its inception, the Christian faith has been interested in the healing of the body and the soul. Many Christians recognize the central place that physical healing took in the earthly ministry of Jesus. Though Jesus as God the Son came to the world on a mission of spiritual healing, he was regularly engaged in helping relieve physical sickness and disease. The Gospels often point out that Jesus's physical healings serve as a visible sign of the authority Jesus has to provide spiritual wellness, including the forgiveness of sins (Matt 9:2–7). However, even with his primary mission being of a spiritual nature, Jesus regularly showed mercy and compassion through physical healings (Matt 4:23–24; 9:27–29, 35–36; John 11:33–36).

The miraculous working of physical healings continued into the ministry of the apostles after Jesus's ascension as a sign to Jews, Samaritans, and Gentiles that the power of Jesus was with them (by the Holy Spirit) and that their gospel message contained the power of God for salvation (Acts 5:12–14; 8:4–8). In the book of Acts, there is somewhat of a shift with the ministry of the apostle Paul. Though his apostolic ministry did include physical healings, he spent much of his time reasoning with Jews and Gentiles from the Scriptures (Acts 14:8–17; 17:1–13) rather than providing physical healing as the main door to further ministry.

While supernatural physical healings became less common in the early church due to those healings being a sign of apostolic ministry (2 Cor 12:12) that ended with the death of the apostles, early Christians were still interested in caring for those who were sick and worked toward restoring physical health. From the second through the fifth centuries, a variety of views of the value of medicine occurred throughout the world, including within Christianity. Some of the leading theologians and pastors of the early church expressed clear support for the value of medicine for physical healing and the valid intersection of faith and medical science. The early Christian teacher Origen debated with a pagan teacher named Celsus on many topics of doctrine. In one part of their debate, Origen noted that different views on certain doctrines existed among Christians just as there were differences of opinion within medical practice. Origen then expressed the ongoing relevance for doctrine and medical practice as being "important and beneficial to human life." Origin writes:

> In reply to which, we say that heresies of different kinds have never originated from any matter in which the principle involved was not important and beneficial to human life. For since the science of medicine is useful and necessary to the human race, and many are the points of dispute in it respecting the manner of curing bodies, there are found, for this reason, numerous heresies confessedly prevailing in the science of medicine among the Greeks, and also, I suppose, among those barbarous nations who profess to employ medicine. . . . And yet no one would act rationally in avoiding medicine because of its heresies [conflicting views].[2]

[2] Origen, *Against Celsus* 3.12, bracketed comment added. For more on early Christian views on faith and medicine, see Darrel W. Amundsen, "Medicine and Faith in Early Christianity," *Bulletin of the History of Medicine* 56, no. 3 (Fall 1982): 326–50, and "Medieval Canon Law on Medical and Surgical Practice by the

Similarly, John Chrysostom, a fifth-century pastor in the capital city of Constantinople, answered pagan critics who believed their superstitious offerings to their gods brought healing while Christians were relying on medical treatment and prayer rather than miraculous healings. Chrysostom noted that healings were not a part of common Christian practice at this point but encouraged the use of medicine for treatment of sicknesses. If those medical treatments failed, then Christians still had the hope of resurrection and life with God. Chrysostom contended that God gave humans medical knowledge so that we would not rely on superstitious practices that claim (wrongly) to help us with physical disease:

> Why, says one, are there not now those who raise the dead, and perform cures? Yes, then, why, I say: why are there not now those who have a contempt for this present life? Do we serve God for hire? When man's nature was weaker, when the Faith had to be planted, there were even many such; but now he would not have us to hang upon these signs, but to be ready for death. Why then do you cling to the present life? Why do you not look to the future? . . . For this cause, it is that there are none such now; because that (future) life hath seemed to us without honor, seeing that for its sake we do nothing, while for this life there is nothing we refuse to undergo. . . . Was it for this that God gave physicians and medicines? What then? Suppose they do not cure him, but the child dies? To where will he depart? . . . Will he not depart to heaven? Will he not depart to his own Lord?[3]

Early Christians valued the use of medicine for the healing of the human body. Early Christians recognized that it was a grace of God to give

---

Clergy," *Bulletin of the History of Medicine* 52, no. 1 (Spring 1978): 22–44; Gary B. Ferngren, "Early Christianity as a Religion of Healing," *Bulletin of the History of Medicine* 66, no. 1 (Spring 1992): 1–15; Rudolph Arbesmann, "The Concept of 'Christus Medicus' in St. Augustine," *Traditio* 10 (1954): 1–28.

[3] John Chrysostom, *Homily 8 on Colossians.*

medical knowledge to humans and for the applications of medicine to bring about the desired healing. Christians have also valued those whose primary work has been serving others through medical care while relying on God to provide ultimate healing. Augustine, a fifth-century pastor in North Africa, relayed this common view of Christians when he wrote, "For as the medicines which men apply to the bodies of their fellow-men are of no avail except God gives them virtue (who can heal without their aid, though they cannot without his), and yet they are applied; and if it be done from a sense of duty, *it is esteemed a work of mercy or benevolence*."[4] As a CHP, you do a work of mercy and compassion with the hope that God will do his work of healing (physical and spiritual) in your patients.

You Are Not Alone—Help from Above

As you start this book and maybe a new journey focused on serving as a Christian in a health-care setting, why don't you pray this prayer?

> *Lord, help me to see my role as a CHP as an important part of my service to others in your name. Help me to rely on you for the hard task of caring for others and for the challenging task of being a vessel of your mercy to others. Help me to see the opportunity of being a Christian serving patients in a health-care setting as something I need to dedicate to you so that your name is honored. I pray, my Father in heaven, that your name would be treated as holy in my life. In the name of Jesus, the Son. Amen.*

Reflection and Discussion Questions

1. We describe Christian health professionals (CHPs) as sharing at least three common features that make us unique—serve on the

---

[4] Augustine, *On Christian Doctrine*, 4.16.33 (emphasis added).

front lines; remind people of their mortality; oaths and professional codes of ethics. Are there other features that distinguish CHPs? Can you list a few others?

2. In your own words, what does it mean to live your life working on the front lines as a CHP? If you are in a class, share with others in small group.
3. We assert that it matters that Lisa Faye, Kevin Salentiny, Pam Carson, Judy Aikens, and Tanya Jordan-Williams are Christian. Can you make the case for or against our assertion? How would you support your perspective?
4. Read through the code of ethics from your profession. Can you articulate some of the standards that cause at least some sense of a dilemma for you navigating life as a CHP?

The next two questions are for student readers:

5. What are the reasons you are pursuing a degree in a health profession?
6. On a scale from 0–10, with 0 meaning no influence and 10 meaning a primary influence, how much do you think you will allow God's Word to shape your professional practice? Can you explain?

The last two questions are for experienced professionals:

7. Perhaps this is the first time you have seriously thought about the integration of your spiritual life with your professional life. Maybe you recently received Jesus as Lord and Savior. What changes now when you work with patients? Can things stay the same? Any changes you need or want to make in your professional life?
8. Every CHP knows that in all areas of health care, there are some mundane and tedious parts of our work. How does God's Word help inform your work during those times?

Chapter 2

God of the Bible

And God is able to make every grace overflow to you, so that in every way, always having everything you need, you may excel in every good work. —2 Cor 9:8

Brenda Wells—Physician and Associate Professor of Internal Medicine

Brenda works at a large teaching hospital in the Midwest. She spends her time equally divided between seeing patients admitted to the hospital and supervising a cohort of second-year residents considering specializing in internal medicine. As part of her supervision, she leads a weekly seminar where she guides residents through patient reviews to determine accurate diagnoses and treatment. Two different patient reviews were described at the last seminar.

The first review was of a nineteen-year-old African American male. Over the past year, the patient has been to several doctors complaining of fatigue, chest pain, and shortness of breath. He also seemed to be having difficulty walking and was experiencing constant tingling in his hands. After several outpatient efforts to treat his different symptoms, the patient was referred to Brenda. She admitted him to the hospital for testing. Given the range of symptoms, she consulted with a pulmonologist, a nephrologist, and someone from oncology. After eliminating the possibility of cancer or kidney disease, it turns out the patient's symptoms were all connected—his issues all stemmed from a late growth spurt. The growth spurt triggered minor pectus carinatum, minimally visible to the naked eye when examined without his shirt. In turn, the pectus carinatum contributed to symptoms of peripheral neuropathy. Treatment involved prescribing a nonsteroidal anti-inflammatory topical medication, discharge from the hospital, and follow-up with an outpatient exam in two weeks. At the follow-up exam, the young man looked like a new person.

The second review was of a fifteen-year-old Caucasian male. The patient had been in the hospital six times in the last eighteen months for a variety of stomach and intestinal related ailments. Each time the patient was admitted to the hospital, the symptoms would subside without the doctors ever really figuring out what was causing this young man so much trouble. During the last hospital admission, while completing a comprehensive social history, the patient finally disclosed to the hospital social worker a repeated history of being sexually assaulted by his uncle. After looking through the treatment notes from the different physicians who treated the young man, Brenda realized that all the physiological symptoms the patient was experiencing were psychosomatic. She ordered the hospital social worker to call child protective services to refer the patient and his family for treatment and investigation.

Understanding the Complete Situation

Brenda presented her students with two complex patient cases. The cases highlighted the need in health-care practice for assessment of different systems of the body as well as environmental factors to provide a complete picture of the situations. In the first case, it seemed the doctors seeing the patient before he was admitted to the hospital were missing something.

They focused on treating the presenting symptoms instead of considering that the symptoms were connected to an underlying condition. It took a multidisciplinary team of physicians to rule out possibilities, discover the primary issue, and treat accordingly.

The second case was causing a conundrum for the doctors as well. There was no apparent reason for the young man to be experiencing so much pain and discomfort. Again, they were missing something. They weren't considering the whole context of the situation. The physical ailments were only part of the story. With the new information, Brenda was able view the stomach and intestinal issues from a broader perspective, realize that the symptoms were all psychosomatic, and get the patient the help he needed from child protective services.

Take a moment to contemplate the cases again. Consider them from a different angle. For instance, what if the medical team in the first case chose to only look at the situation from the perspective of the pulmonologist? What if the team only considered treatment options from the nephrologist who was calling for a kidney biopsy? In the same way, what if Brenda chose to ignore the new information about the second patient? That would be absurd. Instead, she continued ordering expensive and invasive test after test, determined to find the right diagnosis and treat the medical condition. Health-care professionals cannot choose to examine one system of the body while excluding other systems. It is the same for CHPs when we take our relationship with God seriously. We cannot base our relationship with God on specific verses without understanding the context of the verses within the rest of Scripture. Let us provide an example to demonstrate how silly it would be to focus on one verse.

Romans 9:13

In Rom 9:13 Paul writes, "As it is written: I have loved Jacob, but I have hated Esau." Considered by itself, the verse seems to imply that God's love is arbitrary, that God chooses favorites. Can you imagine how pointless it would be to develop your relationship with God based on trying to be his favorite? What a shallow view of God, reducing the almighty Creator of life down to someone who needs to be appeased or impressed. How would that view of God help inform your health-care practice as a Christian? It can't. But, understood within the larger context of Scripture, *thank goodness* God loved Jacob and hated Esau. You see, the verse refers to the nations of Israel and Edom. God chose Jacob and his descendants (Israel) for divine blessing and Esau and his descendants (Edom) for divine judgment. This was God's perfect plan all along.

Paul quotes this verse from Mal 1:2–3 as evidence of God's love for those who come to believe in Jesus Christ as Lord and Savior. In turn, the prophet Malachi refers to the story of Jacob and Esau in Genesis 25 as evidence of God's love for his people apart from any consideration of human effort. It turns out that when considered in the context of the whole Bible, God's love is not arbitrary at all. His love is unconditional as it is based on his sovereign will, revealed in his perfect Word. As such, if CHPs are going to serve the Lord effectively on the front lines, it must come from a comprehensive understanding of God revealed in the complete biblical narrative.

Understanding the Complete Biblical Narrative

God created humans in his image, giving them access to eternal life (through the "tree of life") and a peaceful relationship with him. Through creation, God expresses covenantal love to the first humans and offers them "good" things. God blesses humans as male and female to fill the land and to enjoy the glorious provision of God's beautiful land. God's act of creating humans "like" him means that as humans relate to him, they have the blessings of dominion over creation and priestly service in the land (Genesis 1–2). In other words, humans originally serve as steward-priests who bring glory to God through their management of his creation.

Humans were created for life with God and can make free choices that can honor God. However, through their sinful choice (Genesis 3), the first humans chose death instead of life, foolishness instead of God's wisdom, and sin over righteousness. They were barred from eternal life, and they tainted the image of God. Humans needed another expression of God's covenantal love to be reconciled in their relationship to God and to be made righteous in their standing before him. The human condition is marked with suffering and death due to humanity's sinful disobedience. The bleakness of the human landscape can only be redeemed by a gracious God (Gen 3:15). The story of the Creator-turned-Redeemer becomes the Bible's "big picture" (covenants) and the Bible's "big point" (Christ). As we read through the texts of the Bible, we find out more about how God offers a covenant relationship to humans through the Son (Jesus Christ).

The Bible's Big Picture: Biblical Covenants

The Bible has a remarkable variety of narrative and poetic texts (along with some discourse texts) filled with history, wisdom, commands, and prophetic glimpses of the future. This "book of books" can be framed by six major biblical covenants. These six biblical covenants provide the big picture of Scripture and are the framework of how God pursues a relationship with sinful people. Each of these covenants is introduced in biblical texts, revisited in later biblical texts, and ultimately points to God's gracious work of salvation. They also provide connecting points and a reading guide to biblical books that may seem at first glance to be a bit foreign to us.

The Covenant with Adam (Genesis 1–2)[1]

In Genesis 1–2, humans are created in a relationship with God that takes a form which later is described as covenant. Though there is no explicit

---

[1] See especially Gen 1:26–31 and 2:15–17.

use of the term "covenant" in these two chapters, when compared textually with Genesis 8–9, it is clear that this passage is covenantal.[2] By nature of creation, Adam and Eve have peace in their relationship with God, they have access to eternal life (by eating of the tree of life), and they reflect God's image (Gen 1:26–28). The covenant stipulation is that they not eat of the tree of knowledge of good and evil or they will receive the consequence of covenant breaking: "you will certainly die" (Gen 2:17). The covenant blessings include, "Be fruitful and multiply," dominion over creation, peaceful relationship with God, and trusting God to determine what is "good." The covenant relationship allows these first humans to "worship and obey" the Lord as his beloved creatures, bringing glory to the Creator.[3]

Tragically, the covenant is broken when Adam and Eve's lack of trust causes them to eat of the tree that will give them their own knowledge of good and not good. Unfortunately for their descendants, their "knowledge" of "not good" things will often come through personal experiences, including suffering and death (see Genesis 4–5). Adam and Eve will eventually pass along death, pain, and broken relationships to their children. Strikingly, one of their sons kills his brother, demonstrating how quickly sin spins out of control and how it brings destructive tendencies to the human condition. Amid the curses that result from the fall, a redeemer is promised who will be a descendent (seed) of Eve and will crush the head of the serpent (Gen 3:15). The biblical narratives to follow focus on the descendants of Eve (all humans) as creation awaits the arrival of the "seed" (the Redeemer).

---

[2] See also Hos 6:7 which refers to God's "covenant" relationship with Adam.

[3] See Gen 2:15. "A more suitable translation of the Hebrew text would be 'to worship and obey.' The man is put in the Garden to worship God and obey him. The man's life in the Garden was to be characterized by worship and obedience; he was to be a priest, not merely a worker and keeper of the Garden." John Sailhamer, *The Pentateuch as Narrative* (Grand Rapids: Zondervan, 1992), 101.

The Covenant with Noah (Genesis 6–9)[4]

After the exit from Eden, humans spiraled downward in their evil inclinations. In Gen 6:5, the situation is described in the worst of terms: "When the Lord saw that human wickedness was widespread on the earth and that every inclination of the human mind was nothing but evil all the time." Humanity experiences evil that is widespread because everywhere humans go, they bring this evil in "every inclination of the human mind." This human evil had both spiritual and physical consequences (Gen 6:3). In a surprising contrast to other humans, Noah's faith and obedience are recognized by the Lord (Gen 6:8, 22). In the New Testament, the author of Hebrews describes Noah's faith: "By faith Noah, after he was warned about what was not yet seen and motivated by godly fear, built an ark to deliver his family. By faith he condemned the world and became an heir of the righteousness that comes by faith" (Heb 11:7). Noah's faith becomes the context in which God offers a covenant to humans that will postpone his righteous judgment, providing humans a season of repentance and a chance at life (Gen 6:17–21; see 2 Pet 3:6–9).

After being delivered from the flood, Noah offers a pleasing (faith-filled) sacrifice to the Lord. God responds with a covenant that includes the blessings of "Be fruitful and multiply," dominion over creation, and peace in the relationship with God (the name "Noah" indicates peace/"rest" with God). The blessings of the Noahic covenant reverse aspects of the fall of Genesis 3 (e.g., God will no longer curse the ground due to human sin) and return to some of the blessings of Genesis 1–2 (such as "dominion"), even if slightly modified. However, it is notable that the general human condition as sinful has not changed after the judgment of the flood. Genesis 8:21 says, "When the Lord smelled the pleasing aroma, he said to himself, 'I will never again curse the ground because of human beings, even though the inclination of the human heart is evil from youth onward. And I will never again strike

---

[4] See especially Gen 8:20–9:17.

down every living thing as I have done.'" Though sinful inclinations remain as a characteristic of the human condition, God has extended his mercy by postponing his judgment on sin.

This covenant made with Noah affects all humans by declaring that God will withhold his righteous judgment on human sin in order that humans might have the opportunity to worship him (Isa 54:9–10). However, as human sin persists (see Noah's drunkenness in Gen 9:21–22), covenant renewal is mixed with "curses" and "blessings" (Gen 9:20–29). Generally speaking, human civilization and ingenuity has a tendency to be self-serving instead of reflecting an attitude of stewardship under God (Genesis 11).

The Covenant with Abraham (Genesis 12–17)[5]

Though sin and human pride have created chaos for humans, God decides to act in his mercy by offering a covenant to Abraham (then Abram) in Genesis 12. "The LORD said to Abram: 'Go from your land, your relatives, and your father's house to the land that I will show you. I will make you into a great nation, I will bless you, I will make your name great, and you will be a blessing. I will bless those who bless you, I will curse anyone who treats you with contempt, and all the peoples on earth will be blessed through you'" (Gen 12:1–3).

The blessings of the Abrahamic covenant include: a great land, a great people/nation, and a blessing to all the nations. The promise will be fulfilled in Abraham's descendant ("offspring" in Gen 12:7) and will be repeated among his many descendants.

In Gen 15:3–6, God promises that one of Abraham's descendants ("from your own body") will be the heir to receive God's blessings. The covenant promises of God to Abraham are wrapped up in this heir who will be a blessing to the nations (Gen 12:1–3). Furthermore, the Lord promises more than an heir, but also includes that Abraham's descendants will be as

[5] See especially Gen 12:1–3 and 15:3–6.

numerous as the stars. Abraham believes God's promise about the future heir and the multitude of descendants and is declared to be righteous based on that faith (Gen 15:6).

The *faith* of Abraham is a central part of this covenant. The covenant has an unconditional aspect to the promise, because "the heir" (or offspring from Gen 12:7) will receive God's promise. There is also a conditional aspect to it related to enjoying the blessings. The blessings of the Abrahamic covenant come to those living by faith. The writer of Hebrews points out how through faith Abraham, Sarah, Isaac, and Jacob begin to enjoy aspects of the covenant relationship with God even though the complete fulfillment of the promises will come through a future heir (Christ).

> These all died in faith, although they had not received the things that were promised. But they saw them from a distance, greeted them, and confessed that they were foreigners and temporary residents on the earth. Now those who say such things make it clear that they are seeking a homeland. If they were thinking about where they came from, they would have had an opportunity to return. But they now desire a better place—a heavenly one. Therefore, God is not ashamed to be called their God, for he has prepared a city for them. (Heb 11:13–16)

The Abrahamic covenant is the background (context) for God's gracious dealings with Israel throughout the Old Testament and for his blessings to be extended to the nations (Gentiles) in the New Testament (Rom 4:9–14).

The Covenant with Moses (Exodus 19–20)[6]

In Exod 19:3–8, the Mosaic covenant is presented as a potential fulfillment of the Abrahamic covenant. If Israel fulfills the stipulations of the Mosaic covenant, then it receives the benefits of the Abrahamic covenant,

---

[6] See especially Exod 19:1–9 and Deut 4:1–8.

highlighted by being the people of God as a kingdom of priests. This connection with the Abrahamic covenant implies the requirement of faith for fulfilling the Mosaic covenant. A faithful Israel will be God's chosen people; they will be God's representatives among humans and reserved for God's purposes.

The key stipulation to the Mosaic covenant was faith-filled obedience to God's Word (see Exod 20:1–6). However, before Israel leaves Sinai, they disobey the primary command of the covenant (exclusive worship; see Exodus 32) and therefore break the covenant. In this dismal context, the Lord reveals himself as gracious, abounding in love, and willing to forgive sins. He renews the covenant (Exodus 34), albeit with added stipulations (commands).

The failure of the Mosaic covenant becomes evident through the history of Old Testament Israel. The primary cause of the failure of this covenant is the "heart-problem" of the people, eerily similar to the human condition in Noah's day. The people's hearts are corrupt, and they cannot keep God's commands (Ps 14:1–3; Rom 3:10–12). Though the people are ultimately unable to keep the Mosaic covenant, the reiterated covenant of Exodus 34 is a means of God's gracious blessing to the nation of Israel (Exod 34:10) and his commitment to work among them in a way that is unique to them. From the foundation of the Abrahamic covenant and the renewed Mosaic covenant the Lord gives them the Promised Land (Josh 21:43–45) and raises godly leaders for them (Josh 1:1–18; Judg 10:13–11:27; 1 Sam 7:1–13; see Gen 49:8–10).

The Covenant with David (2 Samuel 7; 1 Chronicles 17)[7]

The ideal godly leader for the nation of Israel is David, the shepherd king. David leads the people to defeat their enemies, but he also leads them to worship the Lord. As David's faith shows through his desire to build a "house" for God, the Lord counters with a promise to David that God will

[7] See especially 2 Sam 7:8–17 (also 1 Chron 17:10–14).

build *him* a house, meaning one of his descendants will be God's great king. The future "son of David" will come and bring the covenant blessings of rest in the land, worship of the Lord, an eternal kingdom, and eternal dwelling in a renewed Jerusalem. One of the chief promises of the covenant is that this coming son of David will be God's Son (1 Chr 17:13; Ps 2:7). The King (Son of David/Son of God) will reign forever over God's people. First Chronicles 17:14 describes God's plans: "I will appoint him over my house and my kingdom forever, and his throne will be established forever."

God's great nation is formed because of the coming King's great kingdom. When he reigns, he establishes the blessings that are promised in the Abrahamic covenant, such as a land of promised peace, a great nation of people, and blessings extended to the nations. The Davidic covenant becomes a new measure of hope to a people who are beleaguered by their disobedience and recurring lack of faith in God.

Old Testament prophecy looks fervently for this coming Son of David. In the Latter Prophets of the OT, the coming Son of David will redeem God's people. As stated in Jeremiah the prophet, "'Look, the days are coming'—this is the LORD's declaration—'when I will raise up a Righteous Branch for David. He will reign wisely as king and administer justice and righteousness in the land. In his days Judah will be saved, and Israel will dwell securely. This is the name he will be called: The LORD Is Our Righteousness'" (Jer 23:5–6).

The recurring themes of hope in the Prophets are that the Lord would remember his covenant promises to Abraham, establish the righteous kingdom promised in the Son of David, and bring new life and forgiveness through the new covenant (Jer 30:3, 9; 31:31–34).

The New Testament Gospel writers picture Jesus as the coming Son of David. It is no wonder, then, that in the genealogy of Matthew 1, Jesus is described as the Son of Abraham and the Son of David. Matthew is pointing out that Jesus is the fulfillment (coming "offspring") of both the Abrahamic covenant and the Davidic covenant. As the Son, Jesus preaches the gospel of the kingdom. The good news of the gospel is that Jesus will provide everything needed to enter the kingdom by offering a new covenant to the people. In Matt 21:9, the crowd shouts this praise to Jesus as the Son of David: "Hosanna, to the Son of David! Blessed is he who comes in the name of the Lord! Hosanna in the highest heaven!"

The New Covenant (Deuteronomy 30; Jeremiah 31; Ezekiel 36; Hebrews 8–10)[8]

The future reign of the Son of David holds all the promise of the formation of a people for God. However, a significant issue remains: human sin and its result, death. The Son of David forms a kingdom of righteousness and peace where all things are made right (justice and healing), but who can belong to such a holy kingdom? The sixth major biblical covenant deals with the problems of sin and death. Through the offer of the new covenant, God promises forgiveness and life. Though it is a new covenant (Jeremiah 31), it is not a new promise. The new covenant is promised even in Moses's last words (Deuteronomy 30), that there will be a circumcision *of the heart*, dealing with an ongoing human problem and the reason for the failure of the Mosaic covenant, sinful disobedience.

Deuteronomy 30 holds out hope for the people because the people *will* be able to obey because their hearts *will* be circumcised. This inward transformation is pictured in Jeremiah 31 as a new heart, and in Ezekiel 36 as a new Spirit. The new covenant will address even the heart. The new covenant is not a renewed version of the Mosaic covenant. The covenant blessings include an internal law, being God's people by the Spirit's work, God's glory being known universally, forgiveness, and a remade promised land.

The one who made redemption is now the mediator of the new covenant (Hebrews 8–10). In Heb 9:15 Jesus's mediating work is described: "Therefore, he is the mediator of a new covenant, so that those who are called might receive the promise of the eternal inheritance, because a death has taken place for redemption from the transgressions committed under

[8] See Deut 30:6–10; Jer 31:31–34; Ezek 36:22–32; Hebrews 8–10.

the first covenant." The new covenant is the means of bringing the blessings of the Abrahamic covenant and the Davidic covenant into actuality (Hebrews 11–12).

Biblical Authors Use the Biblical Covenants as the Big Picture

These six major biblical covenants provide a context for the entire message of the Bible. The covenants interrelate and provide rich biblical imagery for biblical authors to use in later biblical texts. In specific texts or biblical books, the biblical covenants can be in the "background" or in the "foreground," or two covenants can interplay (Luke 1:67–77). For example, a biblical text, like Jeremiah 23, may focus on the sinful actions of humans in light of the commands of the Mosaic covenant ("in the foreground"), while also pointing to a future hope found in the Davidic covenant or the new covenant ("in the background"). What this means is that biblical authors are theologians who help us understand the world and our lives considering God's covenants. The biblical covenants provide a Christological reading for all of Scripture. In other words, as the Bible's big picture the biblical covenants provide the framework for the Bible's big point, Jesus Christ.

The Bible's Big Point: Jesus Christ

Christian Scriptures, the Old and New Testaments, reveal God and his purposes. This revelation is textual in that it is found through reading the Bible. The revelation is also personal because it presents God as he truly is, a personal being. The climax of this personal and textual revelation is the Son. The author of Hebrews notes the significance of the Son to God's Word:

> Long ago God spoke to the ancestors by the prophets at different times and in different ways.
>
> In these last days, he has spoken to us by his Son. God has appointed him heir of all things and made the universe through

> him. The Son is the radiance of God's glory and the exact expression of his nature, sustaining all things by his powerful word. After making purification for sins, he sat down at the right hand of the Majesty on high. (Heb 1:1–3)

The Old Testament (OT) prophets were God's means of speaking to his people, beginning with Moses and continuing through the Latter Prophets of Isaiah, Jeremiah, Ezekiel, and the Twelve.[9] To be more specific, God used the writings of these prophets to reveal his character and purposes, with heightened attention on the promised Messiah. During his earthly ministry, Jesus read and taught the Scriptures (Luke 4:16–21) to the crowds and to his disciples.

Jesus taught that the Hebrew Scriptures were written about him. He and his earliest disciples proclaimed that his life, death, and resurrection on the third day were a fulfillment of the writings of the prophets. In Luke 24, Jesus walked on the road to Emmaus with two disciples who were discouraged because they were struggling to believe the resurrection, in spite of Jesus's regular teaching on it. Jesus corrects them, saying "'How foolish you are, and how slow to believe all that the prophets have spoken! Wasn't it necessary for the Messiah to suffer these things and enter into his glory?' Then beginning with Moses and all the Prophets, he interpreted for them the things concerning himself in all the Scriptures" (Luke 24:25–27). Jesus characterizes the disciples' "slow faith" as an inability to grasp how the OT writings (Scriptures) spoke about him as the Messiah. To help provide them with the needed wisdom of faithful disciples, Jesus interpreted "Moses and all the Prophets" for them, helping them see how "all the Scriptures" spoke about him. Jesus is the Bible's big point.

---

[9] "The Twelve" is a reference to the "Book of the Twelve," also known as the "Minor Prophets."

Later in that same chapter, there is a similar encounter with a larger group of disciples. As that group of disciples are coming to grips with the implications of the resurrection, Jesus gives them some renewed instruction:

> He told them, "These are my words that I spoke to you while I was still with you—that everything written about me in the Law of Moses, the Prophets, and the Psalms must be fulfilled." Then he opened their minds to understand the Scriptures. He also said to them, "This is what is written: The Messiah will suffer and rise from the dead the third day, and repentance for forgiveness of sins will be proclaimed in his name to all the nations, beginning at Jerusalem. You are witnesses of these things." (Luke 24:44–48)

What a remarkable episode. The resurrected Jesus is trying to assure his disciples of God's purposes and give them confidence for the difficult days ahead. How does he assure them? Does he say, "Let me reveal some unknown fact of the universe"? Does he say, "Hey, guys, there is something called DNA"? Does he say, "Let me tell you about this chunk of land that will be known as North America"? No. Instead, to assure his disciples' faith, Jesus leads them in a Bible study. He provides some insights on the Law, Prophets, and Writings (the OT). Jesus speaks about things written about him in those OT texts. Now, in the light of this, the disciples' minds are illumined to understand what those Scriptures were about: Jesus the Messiah. Jesus summarizes the scriptural witness about him in noting three significant events: his suffering, his death, and his resurrection. Those scriptural prophecies have come true in Jesus's life. Even more, his work accomplishes salvation for the nations as people hear with faith the message of the gospel "proclaimed" and then repent of their sins and find forgiveness in Christ. As Jesus concludes his teaching to his disciples, he reminds them that they "are witnesses to these things." Having heard the scriptural message about Christ *from* Christ, these disciples (and all disciples since them) become his witnesses and help neighbors, coworkers, patients, and their families know about the saving work of Jesus.

Not everyone sees that the scriptural prophets were writing about Jesus. Back in John 5, Jesus is being questioned by some skeptical religious leaders. He says that they are refusing to believe the testimonies about him, including that of John the Baptist and the Father's voice from heaven (see Matthew 3). However, he adds one more testimony that they are refusing to believe: the testimony of the Scriptures. Jesus says, "You pore over the Scriptures because you think you have eternal life in them, and yet they testify about me. But you are not willing to come to me so that you may have life" (John 5:39–40). Their refusal to receive him on the basis of the witness of the Scriptures means that they will miss out on eternal life. Jesus drives home his point about the irony of his fellow Jews not believing in him by pointing to the witness of Moses. Jesus questions them, "For if you believed Moses, you would believe me, because he wrote about me. But if you don't believe what he wrote, how will you believe my words?" (John 5:46–47).

Jesus's words are just as staggering now as they were then. In Luke 24 and John 5, Jesus teaches that the OT prophets as far back as Moses were writing about him. Furthermore, he says these ancient texts spoke about his life, death, and resurrection, and that eternal life could be found in believing this message about him. Jesus is not only the Bible's big point, but he is also the main point that we all must grasp if we are going to have life—real life.

The Bible's Big Picture and the Bible's Big Point Offer Life with God

As the OT and NT point our focus on Jesus, the Scriptures are "bearing witness" to him. The Gospel of John speaks of how John the Baptist "came as a witness to testify about the light, so that all might believe" in Jesus, the light. Believing in Jesus gives incredible access to God. Believing in Jesus brings eternal life in God and "the right to be children of God" (John 1:7, 12).

The image of becoming "children of God" is important to understand the Bible's good news. More than just offering long life, the Bible's good news offers relationship with God, life with him. As sinful humans we rebel against God, alienating ourselves from him, but in his grace, he offers a way back to him. In John 14:6, Jesus points to the path: "I am the way, the truth, and the life. No one comes to the Father except through me."

The apostle Paul points to God's gracious work to bring us into fellowship with him through Christ's work on multiple occasions. In one of those texts, 1 Cor 1:9, Paul testifies: "God is faithful; you were called by him into fellowship with his Son, Jesus Christ our Lord." Paul describes God's faithful work as bringing us into "fellowship" with him. Notice also that this relationship comes through Jesus. In this verse, Paul uses four "names" or "titles" to refer to the Savior. He calls him "Son," "Christ," "Jesus," and "Lord." Each of these names gives a glimpse of his person and work.

As the "Son," he is fully God and fully human united in one person serving as the perfect mediator between God and humans. He is the agent of creation and therefore, as creator, rules over all things (John 1:1–14 and Colossians 1). He perfectly fulfilled the will of God (revealed in the Scriptures) even to the point of death. As the resurrected one, he is the head of a new humanity (believers).

As "Christ," he is the promised one of the OT prophets and is "anointed" to be prophet, priest, and king. He reveals God (prophet), sacrificed himself (priest), and will rule over God's eternal kingdom (king). As the promised Messiah, Jesus offers the new covenant to sinful humans, saving them from their sins and restoring relationship with God. By faith in Christ, sinners are united to Christ and begin to share in his benefits, those of the new covenant, such as the indwelling Spirit, eternal life, forgiveness of sins, and a changed heart.

He is "Jesus," which means that he will save his people from their sins (Matt 1:21). The Bible is clear about God's plan of purifying a people for himself through the death of Jesus. In Rev 1:5–6, the apostle John describes how Jesus's blood is central to God's plan of a redeemed people. John writes, "Jesus Christ, the faithful witness, the firstborn from the dead and the ruler of the kings of the earth. To him who loves us and has set us free from our sins by his blood, and made us a kingdom, priests to his God and Father—to him be glory and dominion forever and ever."

The author of Hebrews makes a similar point about God's will of setting apart a people through the body of Jesus. In Heb 10:10, he explains, "By this will, we have been sanctified through the offering of the body of Jesus Christ once for all time." The term "sanctified" or "holy" means that these people have a new identity, a new purpose, and a new relationship with God. Later in chapter 10, Hebrews says that we have access to God's presence through "the blood of Jesus." When these verses call us holy, we might pause and think: *Not me. If my past was known and my darkest sins were revealed, then surely, I could not be called "holy." Maybe God should just use someone else to accomplish his purposes.* If you are thinking that, then listen to these next words from Heb 10:22: "Let us draw near with a true heart in full assurance of faith, with our hearts sprinkled clean from an evil conscience and our bodies washed in pure water." Our deepest rebellions are cleansed and made pure by the blood of Jesus.

The fourth title points to how people become "his people" and have their sins forgiven. He is "Lord." As Lord, he rules over his creation by defeating his enemies and giving life to all those who have found refuge in him. As Paul says in Rom 10:9, "If you confess with your mouth, 'Jesus is Lord,' and believe in your heart that God raised him from the dead, you will be saved." For sinful people, repentance leads to righteousness (Isa 1:27–28) that will characterize the rule of the Son of David (Isaiah 11 and 16). The needed righteousness of the kingdom will only be available to those who seek it (Isa 51:1–5; Zech 8:7–8; Matt 6:33) from the Lord himself, whose righteous reign will be the salvation of his people. God reveals his righteousness in his salvation of his people (Ps 98:1–3). Salvation is needed by all people (Jews and Gentiles) and comes through confessing Jesus as Lord. This truth prompts the church's mission of proclaiming the gospel to all nations.

Relationship with God in Jesus, in spite of our sin, is incredibly good news. Since this news is the Bible's central message, lots of texts point to this hope. However, the Bible also points out two big human problems that could cause us to miss a lasting relationship with God: 1) unbelief, and 2) falling away. Another piece of good news is that God has given us help (or a Helper) to cope with these two big problems.

You Are Not Alone: The Spirit, Our Helper

In the second half of the Gospel of John many of the chapters describe one setting, Jesus's last night with his disciples. He knew that they were still struggling with unbelief about who he really was and—with the trials that were about to happen—that they would be tempted to fall away due to fear or despair. In the last half of John 13, Jesus announces that he is about to leave his disciples and they will not be able to go with him (i.e., his death, resurrection, and ascension). In John 14, Jesus begins with comfort for his disciples' troubled hearts. He says, "Believe in God; believe also in me." To enable their belief, Jesus gives them more words of wisdom and encouragement. He points to his relationship with the Father and how his words and works become the catalyst for their faith. In John 14:15, Jesus encourages feeble-faith disciples with the promise of the Holy Spirit, a comforter and counselor for them. Jesus promises that he will not leave his disciples alone ("as orphans" in John 14:18). In the next few chapters, the Gospel of John describes how the Holy Spirit is God's help to beleaguered disciples. How does the Holy Spirit help us in our relationship with God and in living on mission for him?

The *first help* provided by the Helper, the Holy Spirit, is his presence among us. The New Testament focuses on Jesus's initiation of the new covenant (the Gospels, Hebrews, etc.) which ushers in the age where the Spirit indwells God's people (Acts) and draws the people into relationship with God (Ephesians 1–2; Romans 1–4). The OT prophets promise this same work of the Spirit (Ezekiel 36) in creating relationship with God and enabling obedience to his will. In Romans 8, the apostle Paul explains how the Spirit applies the gospel to the believer, establishing our union with Christ. The Spirit gives life to the believer by leading in godliness and interceding on our behalf (Rom 8:11, 26). In Eph 1:13–14, the Spirit is the down payment of the believer's promised resurrection (our "inheritance"). In short, through the indwelling of the Spirit, God's redeemed people share in the "firstfruits" of salvation now (e.g., forgiveness of sin, new life, a new family) and long for the fulfillment of God's saving promises. These "firstfruits" are not the kingdom because Christ's enemies have not been made his footstool (Psalm 110; Revelation 19–20). One day, every person will recognize him as King (Phil 2:10–11). The firstfruits through the Spirit serve as a witness to us about the coming kingdom, which is fully realized in the new heavens and the new earth with the resurrected people (saints) of God (Revelation 21).

The *second help* provided by the Helper, the Holy Spirit, is the Scriptures. The Spirit inspired the authors of Scripture and guided the preservation of Scripture in the canon. The apostle Peter contends that no prophecy from Scripture originated in human thinking or human intention. Instead, Peter states that the human authors of Scripture give us God's Word as they are "carried along by the Holy Spirit" (2 Pet 1:20–21). The prophets of the OT believed similarly about how the Spirit spoke through the prophets but also warned that the "laws" and "words" in the writings of those earlier prophets had not been heeded because the people "made their hearts like a rock" (Zech 7:11–12). The Spirit's help against this prevailing unbelief and hardened hearts against God's Word is affirmed by Jesus: "But the Counselor, the Holy Spirit, whom the Father will send in my name, will teach you all things and remind you of everything I have told you" (John 14:26).

The *third help* provided by the Helper, the Holy Spirit, is the church, a gathering of God's people. In John 17:20–23, Jesus is praying for his future disciples who will believe through the apostles' testimony. Jesus's prayer for this future church is that they would be unified together with the Father and the Son. Jesus prays, "I am in them and you are in me, so that they may be made completely one, that the world may know you have sent me and have loved them as you have loved me" (John 17:23). Jesus is interceding for the church's unity.

Later, the apostle Paul describes how this church unity comes by the Spirit (Ephesians 4). All who have faith in Jesus receive the Spirit and then are united with other believers into a body, the church (Eph 4:3–6). Paul then extends the metaphor of the church as a Spirit-enabled body to say that Christ is the "head" of this body and that he provides guidance and the strength to minister so that his body serves him. In 1 Corinthians 12, similarly, Paul states that Christians "were all baptized by one Spirit into one body" and that the Spirit empowers the believer with gifts for effective ministry within the life of the body.

These three "helps" from the Spirit mean that we are not alone as we engage in God's purposes. Our personal and professional lives are extensions of the new life we have in Christ that has been enabled by the Spirit's presence in us. The inspired Scriptures give us wisdom and mature our faith so that we think and act more like Jesus. The Spirit-filled church becomes a fellowship of believers on mission together to witness to the hope we have found in Christ. We do not have to be troubled by our difficult circumstances that could prompt despair or fear. We do not have to be troubled by our seemingly feeble faith. We can trust the words and the works of our Savior, Jesus, aided by the Holy Spirit.

Saving Grace and Common Grace

The biblical presentation of salvation is best discovered in the reading (and rereading) of the biblical texts. Throughout the whole canon, narrative books will picture God's saving work in the past in order to stir hope in the climactic salvation in the last days. Further, poetic books in the Bible exemplify people praising God for his great work of salvation and humbling themselves before his righteous judgment.

Before we wrap up this brief overview of the Bible's big picture and the Bible's big point, there is one more Bible text noted above that should get more of our attention. In Exodus 34, Moses has requested to "see the Lord," and though the Lord declines to let him see his face, he does agree to "pass by" Moses, revealing his glory to him. As he passes by, in verses 6–7, the Lord reveals the central aspects of his character and purposes. He says of himself:

> The Lord, the Lord, is a compassionate and gracious God, slow to anger and abounding in faithful love and truth, maintaining faithful love to a thousand generations, forgiving iniquity, rebellion, and sin. But he will not leave the guilty unpunished, bringing the consequences of the fathers' iniquity on the children and grandchildren to the third and the fourth generation.

Here, the Lord indicates that he will do the works of forgiveness and judgment in consistency with his character. His very nature is both faithful love and truth and will prompt his forgiveness and judgment, respectively. His judgment will extend to all who remain in their guilt and will be fitting to the gravity of their rebellion against the holy God. However, the Lord also reveals himself in these verses as a "gracious God."

Because God is a God of grace, he extends the offer of relationship with him. Exodus 34:10 relays how God renews his people through an offer of a covenant that is presented as something similar to a "renewed" version of the Mosaic covenant from Exodus 19–20. As the story of our gracious God continues through the Scriptures, God makes a covenant with people through the new covenant as well. Consistent with his character, the new covenant offers the forgiveness of sins to anyone who repents and believes. Once people receive God's gracious offer of covenant, then they are to be servants or stewards of this grace.

In 2 Corinthians 3, the apostle Paul speaks of the believers in the church at Corinth as being made alive by the Spirit etched "not on tablets of stone but on tablets of human hearts." These two "tablets" are contrasting the Mosaic covenant (tablets of stone) with the work God is doing in his new covenant (tablets of human hearts). Paul explains that the work of God in human hearts is a cooperative service for believers. Paul says that God has given them the competence to be ministers or servants of the new covenant (3:6). To be a servant of the new covenant is to proclaim the gospel, the message of God's saving grace. Ironically, the competence that Paul mentions in chapter 3 is described in chapter 12 as "weakness" because in our weakness God's grace is sufficient and his power is evident (2 Cor 12:9).

Paul makes a similar connection in 2 Corinthians 6 when he says that he and his fellow missionaries are "God's ministers" (6:4). As they serve God, their service is commended by "great endurance, by afflictions, by hardships, by difficulties. . . ." Paul also says, in the context of grace-filled service while suffering, that they will be attended to by "the power of God" (6:7).

Many Christians working in a health-care context can identify with Paul's list of "afflictions, hardships, and difficulties," even if their list is different from his. So, in that challenging atmosphere, the promise of the power of God to accomplish his gracious purposes comforts and encourages. CHPs are often aware of many difficulties and their own weaknesses, so it is satisfying to the weary soul to hear God say, "My grace is sufficient." As servants of the new covenant, CHPs take the message of salvation in Christ into every place they go, whether a work environment or social setting. As servants of God, they minister God's grace to believers and unbelievers by the way they care. Remember—the message of the Bible is that our gracious God has sent his Son into the world as an act of grace and an act of covenant. As servants of this grace, it is a comfort to know that he can extend that grace through us. "And God is able to make every grace overflow to you, so that in every way, always having everything you need, you may excel in every good work" (2 Cor 9:8).

You Are Not Alone: Help from the Past

The eighteenth-century New England pastor, Jonathan Edwards, experienced the frustration of trying to convince people of their need for God and receiving rejection for his troubles. In his work, *On Original Sin*, Edwards identifies the problems of humans as the effect of human sin. He writes, "Thus a propensity attending the present nature or natural state of mankind, eternally to ruin themselves by sin, may certainly be inferred from apparent and acknowledged fact."[10] Because of the sin of Adam ("original sin") shortly after creation, all humanity after him has a default setting to reject the grace of God. This "native corruption" stymies the effects of many gracious acts of God. Edwards argues that God has graciously made himself known broadly (common grace) throughout the ages of history described in the Bible. Edwards says that human depravity profoundly affects humans such that they have rejected God's gracious work. He writes:

> Adam continuing alive near two-thirds of the time that passed before the flood; so that a very great part of those that were alive till the flood, might have opportunity of seeing and conversing with him, and hearing from his mouth, not only an account of his fall, and the introduction of the awful consequences of it, but also of his first finding himself in existence in the new-created world, and of the creation of Eve, and the things which passed between him and his Creator in paradise.[11]

Edwards continues in *On Original Sin* by noting that after the flood with Noah there was much widespread evidence of the destruction that should have been a warning to all the people alive in the decades after the flood. He even adds that God shortens the life of humans (to approximately 100 years) as a means of keeping their mortality before them and helping cultivate a dependence on the living God.[12]

With numerous illustrations drawn from throughout the Bible's storyline, Edwards illustrates the great lengths to which God goes to demonstrate his power, his judgments, or his grace. The scope of God's common

---

[10] Jonathan Edwards, *On Original Sin* in *The Works of Jonathan Edwards*, Volume 3, ed. Clyde A. Holbrook (New Haven: Yale University Press, 1970), 123 (Pt. 1, Ch. 1, Sec. 2).

[11] Edwards, *On Original Sin*, 170 (Pt. 1, Ch. 1, Sec. 8).

[12] Edwards, *On Original Sin*, 171 (Pt. 1, Ch. 1, Sec. 8).

grace is as broad as possible so that all would have a testimony before them. Edwards writes:

> Great things were done in the sight of the nations of the world, tending to awaken them, and lead them to the knowledge and obedience of the true God, in Jacob's and Joseph's time; in that God did miraculously, by the hand of Joseph, preserve from perishing by famine, as it were the whole world; as appears by Gen. 41:56, 57. . . .
>
> After this, in Moses and Joshua's time, the great God was pleased to manifest himself in a series of the most astonishing miracles, for about fifty years together, wrought in the most public manner, in Egypt, in the wilderness, and in Canaan, in the view as it were of the whole world; miracles by which the world was shaken, the whole frame of the visible creation, earth, seas and rivers, the atmosphere, the clouds, sun, moon and stars, were affected; miracles greatly tending to convince the nations of the world of the vanity of their false gods, shewing Jehovah to be infinitely above them, in the thing wherein they dealt most proudly, and exhibiting God's awful displeasure at the wickedness of the heathen world.[13]
>
> When all these things proved ineffectual, God took a new method with the heathen world, and used, in some respects, much greater means to convince and reclaim them, than ever before. In the first place, his people, the Jews, were removed to Babylon, the head and heart of the heathen world (Chaldea having been very much the fountain of idolatry) to carry thither the revelations which God had made of himself, contained in the sacred writings; and there to bear their testimony against idolatry; as some of them, particularly Daniel, Shadrach, Meshach and Abednego,

[13] Edwards, *On Original Sin*, 173 (Pt. 1, Ch. 1, Sec. 8).

> did, in a very open manner, before the king, and the greatest men of the empire, with such circumstances as made their testimony very famous in the world; God confirming it with great miracles; which were published through the empire, by order of its monarch, as the mighty works of the God of Israel, shewing him to be above all gods: Daniel, that great prophet, at the same time being exalted to be governor of all the wise men of Babylon, and one of the chief officers of Nebuchadnezzar's court.[14]

So, in God's great plan, he often sends his people into hostile surroundings so that just in his people's everyday lives and work, his glory would be on display to their unbelieving neighbors (the nations). In other words, God communicates his love, his mercy, and his judgment through his servants of common grace in order that his name be spread throughout his creation. God has revealed himself through his major biblical covenants. Servants of common grace are often the connection point that people have between their existence lived out in the natural (and fallen) world and the gracious promises of forgiveness and new (eternal) life found in Christ through the new covenant. Being aware of God's covenantal love for his creation, CHPs know the Bible's big picture (the covenants) and, as their context allows, can introduce their coworkers and those in their care to the Bible's big point (Jesus Christ).

You Are Not Alone: Help from Above

As you are considering how your work as a CHP may be a means of common grace to one of your patients or coworkers, why don't you pray this prayer with us?

> *Dear Lord, thank you for revealing yourself far and wide so that humans may know you. Please use your words revealed in the Bible to*

---

[14] Edwards, *On Original Sin*, 175 (Pt. 1, Ch. 1, Sec. 8).

help me and those around me to understand that we can be saved from our own sinfulness and unbelief because of the saving work of Jesus. We need to hear from the Bible about the kingdom of your Son and how we can share in this kingdom by faith in him. I pray, heavenly Father, that your kingdom that you revealed throughout the whole Bible would come and be established to your glory throughout the whole world. Let that kingdom, not my own, be the focus of my life now. In the name of King Jesus. Amen.

Reflection and Discussion Questions

1. Describe how the covenants of the Old Testament connect with the new covenant. What is different? What is similar? Try explaining the relationship of the covenants with another believer. See if you can explain things in a concise way free of jargon so that anyone can understand. Now, try explaining the relationship of the covenants to a colleague, a friend, or a family member who you know does not have a relationship with Jesus Christ.
2. What is the Bible's "big point"? What is the purpose of the big point? Practice sharing the answers with another believer. Again, see if you can explain things in a concise way, free of jargon, so that anyone can understand. Now, try sharing the answers with a colleague, a friend, or a family member who you know does not have a relationship with Jesus Christ.
3. How does God ensure that we are not alone? What are the three "helps"? Try explaining how God ensures that we are not alone with another believer.

Chapter 3

Servants of Common Grace

But he said to me, "My grace is sufficient for you, for my power is perfected in weakness." Therefore, I will most gladly boast all the more about my weaknesses, so that Christ's power may reside in me. So I take pleasure in weaknesses, insults, hardships, persecutions, and in difficulties, for the sake of Christ. For when I am weak, then I am strong. —2 Cor 12:9–10

Major (Shelly) Thompson: Air Force Reserve RN: A COVID Mission

After approximately six months of lockdown and life-changing implications, the world operated differently as a result of the COVID pandemic. Major Thompson, an Air Force Reserve Nurse of twelve years, was activated to run a COVID-laden nursing facility, as all the regular nursing home staff were COVID positive and placed in quarantine. Her personal reservations regarding this mission resulted from timing, as this assignment was taking her away from her family for the holidays. Her three adorable children and loving husband would celebrate Christmas and ring in the New Year without their mom and wife.

On December 14, Major Thompson began her first "humanitarian" military journey. After driving four hours on icy roads intensified by poor visibility as a winter storm raged, she arrived at one of the largest nursing home facilities in northern Ohio. Bright and early, 0500 (5 a.m.), Major Thompson reported for duty at the "main entrance" of the nursing home where she processed in and quickly discovered she was the Officer in Charge (OIC) of the west wing, where fifty-seven semi-private rooms housed all COVID-positive nursing home residents.

Major Thompson's skeleton staff consisted of one LPN and three medics, all on military orders, and this mission was also robbing them of familial holiday traditions. Additionally, there was a shortage of guidance on how to organize and provide skilled nursing care to these fifty-seven residents. Major Thompson's orders for the next thirty days were to direct and provide skilled nursing care from 6 a.m. to 6 p.m. She needed to orchestrate a plan to care for her military team and these isolated and lonely long-term-care residents. Assignments were simple: the wing was comprised of three halls, each medic would be responsible for one hall their entire shift—this included providing them with three meals and all personal hygiene needs each day. Major Thompson and the LPN would split the nursing care to provide treatments, medications, and essential therapies. GAME ON.

As the first few days unfolded, it was painfully obvious that, because of isolation needs imposed by an entire population of COVID-positive quarantined residents, every area of "normalcy" was impacted. Supplies, deliveries of food and pharmaceuticals, and disposal of waste was dealt with outside in the frigid cold, making every mundane task monumental. Not to mention the constant personal protective attire further impersonalized every aspect of nursing care Major Thompson embraced.

Within days, Major Thompson came to the realization of the toll caused by this pandemic. Days of isolation imposed by this virus had completely removed family contacts. The residents were declining emotionally, not because of their COVID illness, but because they needed relationships, social interactions, and activities—the comfort of these daily routines no longer existed.

Major Thompson's career was filled with knowledge and expertise. She loved every part of nursing and the opportunities provided daily to care for and nurture patients. This caring and nurturing was rooted in her personal beliefs about God. Each day, Major Thompson was fueled by devotion and prayer. Scriptural leading infused her spirit, which provided joy and strength. This mission was no different. The comfort she received daily lessened the pain of missing her family and was readily passed along to her military colleagues and the residents who had become her temporary family.

In mid-January, as the mission came to an end, Major Thompson reflected on how she attempted to infuse Christ's love and demonstrate servant leadership in every interaction. Each situation, no matter how big or small, presented an opportunity to be salt and light and share God's love. Nursing was her Christian vocation where she served patients as a servant of common grace.

Two Journeys, One Vocation

Major Thompson seemed to integrate seamlessly her training as a nurse and her relationship with Jesus to care for patients and her colleagues. What appeared so natural, however, was the fruit harvested from a life committed to professional training and spiritual growth. The two lifelong journeys must converge for CHPs to live into their Christian vocation. Let's take a closer look at her journey.

Her Professional Journey

Before she was Major Thompson, Shelly likely began her professional journey as a teenager. Her journey of becoming a health professional would be all-encompassing. Having the aptitude and desire to help people is just the beginning. Her journey consisted of years of education, years of sacrifice, and years of training. She likely engaged in long hours of studying and in clinical rotations for little to no pay. After graduation, the learning and training actually never ended. She had to study and pass licensure exams, complete continuing education, and keep abreast of the latest in literature. Then there was her military training preparation. She endured officer training school and must continue to report for training one weekend per month and two weeks every summer. When she is not serving as a reserve officer, Shelly probably works somewhere else as a civilian. Finally, beyond her professional responsibilities, she likely has a family and a personal life that she cares about living.

All of her responsibilities as a CHP make her journey lifelong. The potential for burnout is real. As an experienced CHP, she knows exactly why so many of her colleagues have troubled personal lives, turn to destructive addictive behaviors to cope, or disengage from really caring about patients just to survive. To thrive, she needs to be intentional about another lifelong journey.

Her Spiritual Journey

The way Shelly integrated her faith with her practice is evidence of an intentional spiritual journey. It would be fascinating to hear about her relationship with God. How and when did she confess her sins and receive Jesus Christ as Lord and Savior? Did she come to know Jesus as a child or later as an adult? How does she spend her time growing in her relationship with him? Does she delight in reading God's Word? How would she describe her prayer life? What have been some of the joys and blessings she has experienced? What were some of the trials and sufferings she endured? How has her relationship with God sustained her in the past? How does he sustain her now? How does her relationship with Christ inform her life as a nurse? Did she have mentors who provided discipleship for her life on the front lines as a CHP? Does she now mentor other younger CHPs in their faith and in their professions?

Your Professional Journey

What about your professional journey? If you are a student, can you envision the path ahead? You are probably thinking about navigating through various stages of education. There are always certain classes everyone dreads and must endure. Maybe you're in the midst of completing an internship or a clinical rotation, while also taking classes. Are you thinking about graduate school, or getting a job? Do you have an idea of the area of health care you are interested in pursuing? If you are an experienced professional, do you remember your journey so far? Are you having thoughts of changing directions, perhaps pursuing a different area of practice? Have you experienced a season in the desert where the passion and the zeal faded, at least for a time? Almost every CHP has thought about quitting at some point. Have you? What keeps you going? Do you remember why you chose to pursue serving people in health care in the first place? Can you find your way back to being effective on the front lines again? What about your spiritual journey?

Your Spiritual Journey

Your spiritual journey will shape the level of convergence with your professional journey. Just as God constantly reveals in Scripture how important it is to remember who God is, what he has done, and what he will do, we believe it is important for you to reflect consistently upon your testimony. Do you remember what you were like before entering a relationship with Jesus Christ? Do you remember what God says happened to you when you confessed your sins and believed in his Son as Lord and Savior? Reflect on the spiritual transformation that happened, *and is now happening*, in your life. Think about the highest of highs you have experienced so far as a Christian. Think about the lowest of lows. What are some of the essential lessons from Scripture that sustain you? What is God doing in your life right now? Where are you supposed to serve him?

Maybe you are an experienced health professional who recently received Jesus as Lord. The same questions are relevant for you as well. What does your relationship with the Lord mean for your practice? The Holy Spirit will likely press upon you to begin contemplating almost everything you do in health care. What happens to you now? God may call you to something new. He may call you to remain where you are, doing what you are doing, but change the reasons you are there at the front lines. The next few months and years are critical. If you are reading this book, we want you to avoid the temptation to compartmentalize your spiritual life from your professional life. Instead, let your new relationship with Jesus inspire you to embrace your Christian vocation.

Christian Vocation

When CHPs actively invest in their relationships with Jesus Christ, they will need to live one integrated life. It will become impossible for them to keep their personal, professional, and spiritual lives separate forever. The Holy Spirit will make the desire and need for biblical integration unavoidable.

CHPs can try, for a season, to compartmentalize their lives. If they do, they will likely experience pain and suffering without any joy. In our (Angie and Michael) experience, disconnecting faith from your practice results in the following consequences. Your faith life will suffer as you will likely be spending less time in God's Word, less time with him in prayer, and less time in discipleship with others. Your professional life will suffer as your practice will become a means to an end, you will likely get burned out from the endless patients who need your care and the administrative bureaucracy causing you stress. Your personal life will suffer as the joy from your work will be gone, the likelihood of experiencing situational depression and anxiety will increase, and you will just not be a pleasant person to be around.

The opposite will happen when you are deliberate about integration. Biblical integration *will* result in you embracing your Christian vocation. By "Christian vocation," we mean your divine calling where your faith in and devotion to Jesus Christ find mature fulfilment. Christians, regardless of their profession, must wrestle with the concept of calling. From a theological perspective, Christians have a primary and a secondary calling. The primary calling is to glorify God in all things, at all times, forever. The secondary calling is to steward our gifts, talents, and resources to serve God and others. When your primary and secondary callings have a significant nexus with your occupation, it opens the door to pursue your vocation as a part of your occupation. Now being a nurse, a social worker, a doctor, or any other health professional becomes more than a career; it becomes a part of your divine calling. Your divine calling as a CHP is to serve God in health care as one of his servants of common grace.

Servants of Common Grace

The divine calling as servants of common grace unifies every CHP. A relationship with God transforms what you do in health care beyond specific professional backgrounds, places of practice, and particular roles and tasks. Your work can be a testimony that God is the Creator and Sustainer of all things and that his revealed Word is true. As you care for patients on the front lines, remind them of their mortality, and abide by professional ethics, you personify common grace.

What Is Common Grace?

Common grace is a theological term. Different from saving grace (by which God rescues believers in Jesus Christ from the penalty and power of sin and guarantees salvation), the term describes the goodness and kindness of God to all humanity. Stated differently, whereas saving grace is exclusive to people who believe in Jesus as Lord and Savior, common grace is a gift of God available to any person regardless of faith status, geography, or ethnicity.[1] Common grace stems from two theological truths. First, God is a good and gracious creator. So he acts in consistency with his character when he bestows good things on his creatures. Second, God created humans in his image and in relationship to him (Genesis 1–3). His eternal plan is to restore believing humanity to that image and relationship. His common grace is the good means that he uses to preserve and protect humans throughout time as creation waits for God's final acts to come to fulfillment. There are many passages in the Bible that demonstrate the common grace of the Lord. Here are a few examples from the Old Testament and the New Testament.

Genesis 2:15–17; 3:14–24

When God created Adam and Eve, he took them and placed them in the garden of Eden. He gave them their purpose to worship and obey the Lord by working and keeping it (Gen 2:15). He then commanded them that they were allowed to eat from every tree in the garden except one. God spoke to them saying, "You are free to eat from any tree of the garden, but you must not eat from the tree of the knowledge of good and evil, for on the day you eat from it, you will certainly die" (vv. 16–17). But what happened in the next chapter? Did Adam and Eve die the very moment they ate fruit from the tree of knowledge of good and evil? Let's read what God does with their direct disobedience, their unholiness:

---

[1] For further reading on common grace: Jochem Douma, *Common Grace in Kuyper, Schilder, and Calvin: Exposition, Comparison, and Evaluation*, trans. Albert H. Oosterhoff and ed. William Helder (Hamilton, ON: Lucerna CRTS, 2017). See also John MacArthur and Richard Mayhue, *Biblical Doctrine: A Systematic Summary of Bible Truth* (Wheaton: Crossway, 2017), 487–89. Also, see Wayne Grudem, *Systematic Theology: An Introduction to Biblical Doctrine* (Grand Rapids: Zondervan, 1994), 657–68.

> So the LORD God said to the serpent: "Because you have done this, you are cursed more than any livestock and more than any wild animal. You will move on your belly and eat dust all the days of your life. I will put hostility between you and the woman, and between your offspring and her offspring. He will strike your head and you will strike his heel."
>
> He said to the woman: "I will intensify your labor pains; you will bear children with painful effort. Your desire will be for your husband, yet he will rule over you."
>
> And he said to the man, "Because you listened to your wife and ate from the tree about which I commanded you, 'Do not eat from it': The ground is cursed because of you. You will eat from it by means of painful labor all the days of your life. It will produce thorns and thistles for you, and you will eat the plants of the field. You will eat bread by the sweat of your brow until you return to the ground, since you were taken from it. For you are dust, and you will return to dust."
>
> The man named his wife Eve because she was the mother of all the living. The LORD God made clothing from skins for the man and his wife, and he clothed them. The LORD God said, "Since the man has become like one of us, knowing good and evil, he must not reach out, take from the tree of life, eat, and live forever." So the LORD God sent him away from the garden of Eden to work the ground from which he was taken. He drove the man out and stationed the cherubim and the flaming, whirling sword east of the garden of Eden to guard the way to the tree of life. (Gen 3:14–24)

Adam and Eve, representing all of mankind, deserved immediate, physical death for their disobedience to God. In an instant they became unrighteous and unholy, unable to live in the presence of the Lord. They were spiritually dead. They had lost the life and relationship that they had in God through his creating them in his image. In their foolishness and pride, they let sin into the world. Justice warranted their swift execution. Take a moment to think about the point we are making. Had God given Adam and Eve the entirety of the punishment they deserved, there would be no world as we know it. Adam and Eve would have experienced the ultimate consequences for letting sin into the world. But God did not execute them right away, and that gracious pause would make all the difference.

Instead, God pronounced his curse on Satan, promised victory over sin through his Son, and pronounced his curse on the ground due to Adam and Eve's sin. He then removed them from the garden of Eden. They were exiled but breathing. God extended to Adam and Eve a temporary stay of execution. Though they would eventually die, in his mercy, God suspended the consequences of sin. He allowed them to live for centuries and gave them time to reproduce. God's extension of life, which made redemption possible, is his free gift of common grace to all of humanity.

Genesis 8:20–9:17

In a later setting of sin and disobedience, God again intersperses his judgment with his grace. At the end of Genesis 8, the Lord establishes his covenant with Noah. Let's read what God promises him:

> Then Noah built an altar to the LORD. He took some of every kind of clean animal and every kind of clean bird and offered burnt offerings on the altar. When the LORD smelled the pleasing aroma, he said to himself, "I will never again curse the ground because of human beings, even though the inclination of the human heart is evil from youth onward. And I will never again strike down every living thing as I have done. As long as the earth endures, seedtime and harvest, cold and heat, summer and winter, day and night, will not cease."
>
> God blessed Noah and his sons and said to them, "Be fruitful and multiply and fill the earth. The fear and terror of you will be

in every living creature on the earth, every bird of the sky, every creature that crawls on the ground, and all the fish of the sea. They are placed under your authority. Every creature that lives and moves will be food for you; as I gave the green plants, I have given you everything. However, you must not eat meat with its lifeblood in it. And I will require a penalty for your lifeblood; I will require it from any animal and from any human; if someone murders a fellow human, I will require that person's life. Whoever sheds human blood, by humans his blood will be shed, for God made humans in his image. But you, be fruitful and multiply; spread out over the earth and multiply on it."

Then God said to Noah and to his sons with him, "Understand that I am establishing my covenant with you and your descendants after you, and with every living creature that is with you—birds, livestock, and all wildlife of the earth that are with you—all the animals of the earth that came out of the ark. I establish my covenant with you that never again will every creature be wiped out by floodwaters; there will never again be a flood to destroy the earth."

And God said, "This is the sign of the covenant that I make between me and you and every living creature with you, a covenant for all future generations: I have set my bow in the cloud, and it shall be a sign of the covenant between me and the earth. Whenever I form clouds over the earth and the bow appears in the clouds, I will remember my covenant between me and you and all the living creatures: water will never again become a flood to destroy every creature. The bow will be in the clouds, and I will look at it and remember the permanent covenant between God and all living creatures on earth." God said to Noah, "This is the sign of the covenant that I have established between me and every creature on earth." (Gen 8:20–9:17)

Life before the flood reeked from the consequences of sin entering the world. The descendants between Adam and Noah created a violent, brutal, desolate existence. The wickedness and corruption got so bad that God even grieved and lamented that he made humans and put them in the land (Gen 6:6). Life after the flood reset the current development of humanity. God pushes back future judgment as a measure of common grace to all humans. Second Peter 3:6–9 notes that this grace was another instance where God "is patient with you." Here again, the covenant with Noah is evidence of God's free gift of common grace as a new order of things inclusive of all human beings. Seedtime and harvest, cold and heat, summer and winter, day and night now continue for everyone until the end of the world. God blessed humans to be fruitful and multiply, gave us dominion over every living thing, and holds us all accountable for how we value human life because humans were made in his image.

John 1:1–5, 9

Because God is the Creator of all things, he relates to all things and all people through the lens of his grace. At the beginning of the Gospel of John, we see God's grace toward all in his creating work. As God the Word (the Son, Jesus) was active in creation which brings life to the world, Jesus will bring eternal life to anyone who believes. Notice how in the verses below the blessing of life for all humanity is rooted in Jesus Christ. Read how John describes Jesus Christ.

> In the beginning was the Word, and the Word was with God, and the Word was God. He was with God in the beginning. All things were created through him, and apart from him not one thing was created that has been created. In him was life, and that life was the light of men. That light shines in the darkness, and yet the darkness did not overcome it. (1:5)

And a few verses later John writes:

> The true light that gives light to everyone was coming into the world. (v. 9)

As God the Son, Jesus is the agent of creation. John 1 is reflecting back on Genesis 1. The Son is the Word of God and was with God. He causes all things to exist. He is the source of life. He gives light to *everyone.* The point John is making here is that just as the Son (as Creator) is responsible for the physical life of all humans, so he (as Redeemer) will bring spiritual life to anyone who receives him (John 1:12) through a spiritual (not physical) birth (John 1:13).

Because of God's gracious creation through the Son, all people live in the world and the light designed by God. Please understand that with sin entering the world, his light was and is the only thing that stands in the way of utter darkness. By utter darkness we mean no life, no marriage, no art, no science, no food, no pleasure, no love, and for our purposes, no health care. Just death and darkness. God through the Son causes all that we consider good and virtuous to exist.

Ultimately, John tells us that when Jesus, the light, enters the world, he is rejected by his own (John 1:10–11). Due to persistent unbelief, the gospel message about Jesus must be believed. According to the Gospel of John, the light of the Son is spread to humans through the spoken word (see the testimony of John the Baptizer in John 1:6–8). This preaching is available to everyone and is a part of God's free gift of common grace. However, to have true spiritual life, humans need the power of saving grace. Common grace gives fallen humanity access to some knowledge of God, but not extending to salvation. As the Gospel of John continues, Jesus warns that those who hear the message about him and do not believe will face judgment and will increase in their animosity toward him and the truth that he presents. While it is God who calls sinful humans by his saving grace to know Jesus Christ as Lord and Savior, the testimony about the life of Jesus found in the Gospels (and shared in the testimonies of CHPs) is a part of God's grace that can reach all humans.

Romans 1:18–23; 2:14–15

The connection and distinction between common grace and saving grace is on full display in the book of Romans. Paul presents the doctrinal truth that the righteous shall live by faith (Rom 1:17; Hab 2:4). He then spends the next few chapters (the rest of Romans 1 through Rom 3:20) correcting everyone attempting to have a relationship with God apart from grace alone, through faith alone, in Christ alone. As Paul carefully draws out the distinction between the law and the gospel, evidence of common grace is clear and obvious. Read what God inspires Paul to write:

> For God's wrath is revealed from heaven against all godlessness and unrighteousness of people who by their unrighteousness suppress the truth, since what can be known about God is evident among them, because God has shown it to them. For his invisible attributes, that is, his eternal power and divine nature, have been clearly seen since the creation of the world, being understood through what he has made. As a result, people are without excuse. For though they knew God, they did not glorify him as God or show gratitude. Instead, their thinking became worthless, and their senseless hearts were darkened. Claiming to be wise, they became fools and exchanged the glory of the immortal God for images resembling mortal man, birds, four-footed animals, and reptiles. (Rom 1:18–23)

Common grace is the recognition that God leaves his imprint on his handiwork. That there is a power and a being greater than humans should be evident in what God made (e.g., life in creation). When human beings do not acknowledge God, it is because of unrighteousness suppressing the truth about him. But make no mistake, the external creation of the world and our own internal conscience verify that he is real. We are all without excuse. Common grace is present even when people become fools by exchanging the glory of God for images. When people worship images (idols) instead of God, they still display the residue of the divine impulse to worship something. For our purposes, the desire for good health demonstrates how far God's grace reaches. Even the atheist, when he or she desires healing from an illness or injury, is not merely seeking survival as if it were an instinctual response to an affliction. No, they engage in idol worship as they consciously seek to be restored to what they envision as being well.

In chapter 2 of Romans, Paul writes, "So, when Gentiles, who do not by nature have the law, do what the law demands, they are a law to themselves even though they do not have the law. They show that the work of the law is written on their hearts. Their consciences confirm this. Their competing thoughts either accuse or even excuse them" (2:14–15).

The desire to do good and follow the law is evidence of common grace. God's free gift of common grace exists as he leaves some residue of his reality and his law in the hearts of fallen sinners. When people, regardless of their beliefs about Jesus Christ, by nature do what the law requires, it validates Paul's claim that the work of the law remains on their heart. When people are moved to do good or refrain from evil, promote justice, protect against injustice, empathize and provide care for the sick and suffering, their conscience and thoughts reflect the reality that God exists. Consider Paul's words from a different angle. The residue of God's reality and his law is essential, as the world would quickly spiral into chaos without it. There is no good news, no preaching the Word of God, no sharing the testimony of Jesus Christ, without his common grace.

Purposes of Common Grace

CHPs serve people for reasons beyond immediate healing and relief. God uses your interactions with patients to accomplish at least three purposes of common grace.

As a CHP, you prevent patients from experiencing the complete consequences of their sin. You are faced with a sobering reality. If God allowed patients to experience the full weight of their sin, they would surely die. When you care for patients, you make God's presence known by preventing them from experiencing the complete consequences of their depraved existence. Through common grace and competent training, you work to extend their lives, giving them more opportunities to recognize the grace of God. Patients come to see us because they know something is not right, they are trying to prevent something unpleasant from happening to them, or they need our help in the midst of anguish. Whatever they are experiencing, it is but a foretaste of the full manifestation of their sin. *And their consciences know it*. At the front lines, reminding them of their mortality, CHPs help patients cope with their consciences as we seek to heal their minds and bodies.

As a CHP, you enable patients to experience temporary goodness and peace. Common grace enables believers and unbelievers alike to experience temporary physical blessings from God. When patients are injured or feeling sick and we use the necessary treatments and medications that make them well, we provide undeniable evidence of God's gracious provision to every man and woman. When we examine patients, check their breathing, their blood pressure, and their pulse, we confirm for them that the breath of life from God, the only reason they are alive, remains in them until they return to dust. In the same way, when we help patients experience renewed hope from their addictions or their mental and emotional pain, their temporary joy and wholeness provides evidence of the abundant loving-kindness of the Lord, though only a glimmer compared to the permanent restoration that comes from believing in the gospel of Jesus Christ.

As a CHP, you keep patients alive and healthy as long as possible to hear the gospel. But have you ever paused to ask, "Why?" Say, for instance, you work primarily with children or adolescents. You might answer that your purpose is to help them grow up to be healthy adults. But healthy for what? A good job, a family, a home? Are those really the reasons for serving patients? While it is a good thing to help recover their functionality for family relationships and societal contributions, is that enough to sustain you in your practice on the front lines? Can that be the reason God has equipped you with the ability and drive to be a CHP? Consider a different question and angle: As a CHP who has taken an oath to provide care and seek the best well-being for patients, will providing temporary health be enough? How can you practice without pointing patients to the cross? The answer is that as a servant of common grace, serving patients on the front lines, a significant purpose is to keep patients alive and functioning long enough so that they might hear the gospel, confess and repent of their sins, and receive Jesus Christ as Lord and Savior.

It Is All God's Grace

Students often ask us (Michael and Angie) if it is okay to pray with clients. They want to know if it is ethical to share about their relationship with Jesus Christ with patients and colleagues. Some wrestle with if it is even possible to uphold the code of ethics from their respective professions while remaining steadfast to a biblical worldview. There seems to be a never-ending search for conceptual boundary lines to help CHPs know when they are getting too close. Then there is the fear of crossing the lines and facing the consequences. We can all envision worst-case scenarios of losing our jobs and our licenses to practice. It has been our experience that students and colleagues spend too much time trying to navigate when and how we incorporate our beliefs into our health-care practice. Our encouragement is to instead shift the depth and breadth of our approach by understanding the relationship between common grace and saving grace.

Here is perhaps the most important point of the book—*There is only one grace.* It is all God's grace manifested in two separate ways, used in divine perfection, accomplishing the same victory. God's common grace accomplishes the purposes we describe above. His saving grace is how God rescues those who believe in the Son from the penalty of sin and regenerates and sanctifies them through the work of the Holy Spirit, sealing them for eternity.

You are *always* proclaiming your relationship with Jesus Christ. Just as other believers, CHPs are "a chosen race, a royal priesthood, a holy nation, a people for his own possession, that you may proclaim the excellencies of him who called you out of darkness and into his marvelous light" (1 Pet 2:9). In a real sense, CHPs are actually all servants of grace, just functioning most often as servants of common grace. This changes everything for you. Pursue and embrace your profession seeking to always proclaim your relationship with God. If you do, God will transform *everything*. The challenging cases, the long hours, the mundane tasks, the colleagues that drive you crazy, the policies that sometimes seem to impede the best patient care, God has you there representing him as his servants of grace.

Practice Behaviors for Servants of Common Grace

We sought to meet two objectives in the last three chapters. We want you to recognize your occupation as potentially a part of your vocation. Whatever health-care field you identify with, however recent or long ago you placed your faith in Jesus Christ, you now serve God in your occupation as a Christian health professional (CHP), making your work a part of your vocation. We also want you to embrace your purpose. Wherever you work in health care, however you care for patients, your role is to represent God as a servant of common grace. Before moving on to the next section, we need to address one more thing. Using terminology familiar to health professionals, we need to consider the practice behaviors that contribute to developing competence as servants of common grace.

How we develop professional competence and competence as servants of common grace are different. On one hand, increasing professional competence happens as we continue training, gaining experience, learning new techniques, and staying abreast of the latest developments in our respective fields. On the other hand, God gave us the Holy Spirit who wills us to fulfill our purpose as servants of common grace. Certain practice behaviors, however, help align us with God's purposes. Below are five practice behaviors every CHP should resolve to make a priority. Moreover, if you are feeling overwhelmed, exhausted, or burned out, we encourage you to incorporate these five practice behaviors. Invest time in these practice behaviors instead of turning to unhealthy outlets or before making any drastic decisions about the future. Give God the opportunity to transform your practice.

Consistent Time in His Word

Listen to us . . . *THE* most important thing you can do as a CHP is to practice spending consistent time with God in his perfect Word. The extent to which you will be prepared for God to transform your interactions with patients and colleagues into opportunities for ministry hinges on you having an active relationship with Jesus Christ through his Word. The only way you thrive and endure on the front lines is through a dynamic relationship with God through his Word. Are we stating it clearly enough? Sure, every Christian should spend consistent time in the Scriptures, but your vocation as a CHP requires God's Word to be the first book of your heart and soul. Commit to viewing God's Word this way. It is the Bible and then the *Physicians' Desk Reference*. It is the Bible and then the *Diagnostic and Statistical Manual of Mental Disorders*. It is the Bible and then *Therapeutic Modalities for Musculoskeletal Injuries*. It is the Bible and then the *Atlas of Human Anatomy*.

Saturate your heart and mind in God's Word. Let his Word give you the wisdom to make sense of everything else you need to learn and do as a CHP. Here is what is really amazing about spending time with God through the Scriptures. He will bless you and mold you and transform you through a few dedicated minutes with him every day. One approach is to read a few verses or a chapter of the Bible as the last thing you do before going to bed and/or the first thing you do when you wake up in the morning. For those of you who want and yearn for more, purchase a study Bible that will provide insightful commentary and relevant applications of what you are reading each day. Engage in a discipleship relationship with another Christian, maybe even another CHP, to spend an hour each week studying

God's Word together. Whatever you do, keep it simple. Just rejoice and delight knowing that God, the Creator of everything, invites you to have an intimate fellowship with him through Jesus Christ.

Prayer

CHPs need active prayer lives. Through Jesus Christ, God gifts us the ability to have personal communication with him. When CHPs pray, we share all of ourselves with God and he reinforces all of who he is with us. Prayer helps us remember to trust and depend on the Lord, and it allows us to humble ourselves and cast all our worries on him. It is through prayer, asked in faith, that God transforms your interactions with patients and colleagues. Prayer is one way God reminds you of your involvement in the work of his kingdom. It is the only way you can hope to grasp the magnitude of fulfilling a role that has eternal significance.

Prayer is a means of sanctification (i.e., maturity of faith). Your maturity as a believer goes hand-in-hand with thriving and enduring as a servant of common grace. In the following chapters we turn our attention to the biblical practices that characterize the various things you do as a servant of common grace. We also explore prayer in more depth in the last chapter of the book. For now, it will suffice for us to share that the health of your prayer life will influence the fruit of those biblical practices. If you have not done so already, we invite you to begin praying right now. Put the book down. Close your eyes. Bow your head. Take a few minutes . . . If you want, pray with us now:

> *Lord, thank you for all that you created. May your will be done on earth as it is in heaven. If it is your will, Lord, allow us to represent you well—let us be your ambassadors with every patient and colleague we work with. Through your Holy Spirit, give us the wisdom to use all of our time as an opportunity to bear fruit as a follower of your Son. Help us trust you for our daily bread and our daily strength. Give us patience with ourselves as you transform us more and more into effective servants*

of grace. Lord, bless the ministry of every CHP serving you on the front lines in matters of life and death. Help sustain them when they are weak. Help them to rejoice in all that you call them to do. Help them find solidarity as they discover other CHPs serving alongside them. We ask all this in the name of Jesus Christ. Amen.

Joining a Local Church

CHPs need to belong to a good local church. There are lots of things you can do when away from the front lines. Make it a priority to participate in the life of a vibrant church, one where you can worship with fellow believers, develop discipleship relationships with other members, and learn from the sound teaching and preaching of God's Word. There are a few ecumenical signposts to look for in any good local church. Everything the church does should be centered on the gospel of Jesus Christ. The church leaders should have taken the time to articulate exactly what they believe about sound biblical doctrine. The pastors should preach sermons from the biblical text week after week. Those sermons should tie into the complete biblical narrative of the gospel of Jesus Christ often—perhaps every week. The songs of the church should help you rejoice, help you repent, and help you lament as someone who depends on the Lord. Commit yourself to the other believers there by going through the membership process. The church should be filled with leaders and laypeople who, regardless of diverse backgrounds, exude a culture of grace and love, while also practicing biblical church discipline. There are no perfect churches, and churches can change over time. Participate in church as someone who spends consistent time in God's Word and in prayer so you can discern the presence of the signposts.

Engaging the Word-Centered Contemplative Cycle

Practice engaging the Word-centered contemplative cycle. As you invest in your relationship with God, let that relationship influence your training and practice as a CHP. Likewise, submit all of your training and practice as a CHP under the truth of his inerrant Word (See Figure 3.1).

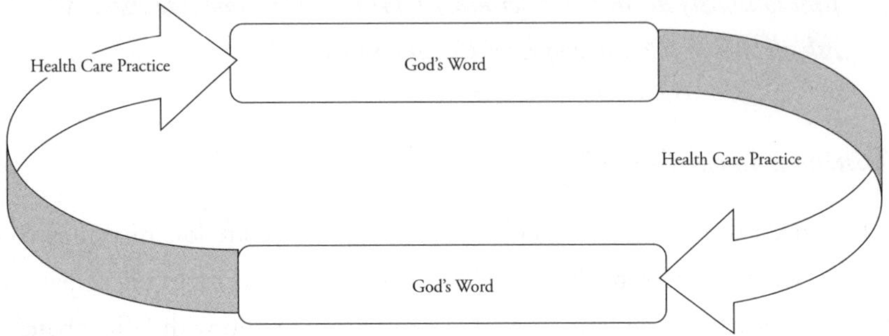

Figure 3.1 Contemplative Cycle to Inform Your Training and Your Practice

If you have never thought to integrate your Christian life with your health profession, this will take deliberate effort at first. In time, if you are consistent, you will begin to reflect effortlessly upon what you're doing through a biblical perspective—which will bear fruit in your practice with patients and colleagues. The Word-centered contemplative cycle is how the two lifelong journeys of professional training and spiritual growth converge. This Word-centered contemplative cycle can provide the strength and courage needed for each choice and act of service as a CHP. For a biblical example, see Josh 1:6–9. It is how Major Thompson seemed to seamlessly integrate her training as a nurse and her relationship with Jesus to care for patients and her colleagues. It will also help you become an effective servant of common grace as it will keep you attuned to your development as a disciple of Jesus Christ, which only happens through Spirit-powered obedience.

Spirit-Powered Obedience

It is the indwelling of the Holy Spirit that brings you closer in your relationship with Jesus Christ. God always moves first. God puts the desire in our heart to spend time with him in his Word. God gives us the desire to spend time with him in prayer and to worship with others at church. God gives us the knowledge and wisdom to discern how to live out our faith as CHPs. Our role is to respond in active Spirit-powered obedience.

The practice of responding in active Spirit-powered obedience is progressive as you mature in your faith. The Holy Spirit inspires you to lay down your flesh, pick up your cross, and become more like Jesus Christ every day. Paul writes, "I say, then, walk by the Spirit" (Gal 5:16a). He then writes, "If we live by the Spirit, let us also keep in step with the Spirit" (v. 25). The more you follow him, the more he gives you to follow. The progression of your obedience will then seamlessly influence every part of your practice. It will happen in your direct interactions with patients and colleagues. It will happen in the indirect decisions you make about your profession. For example, as you keep in step with the Spirit, more and more patients and colleagues will trust you with what is really going on in their lives. Likewise, the Holy Spirit will empower you with the discernment to make decisions about where you work, to navigate relationships with supervisors and insurance companies, and to know when to say yes or no to professional opportunities. Discerning when to say yes or no is important because as you stay in step with the Spirit, your opportunities for sharing grace through words and actions will increase exponentially. Notice again the example of Joshua in Deut 34:9: "Joshua son of Nun was filled with the spirit of wisdom because Moses had laid his hands on him. So the Israelites obeyed him and did as the Lord had commanded Moses."

An Invitation to Become a Servant of Common Grace

Do not put your relationship with Jesus Christ on cruise control. Do not leave God at home when you work in health care. It is too much for you to handle on your own. You will either burn out, experience anxiety, or turn to destructive vices to cope. Instead, make the five practice behaviors a priority for your life. Accept God's invitation to transform your practice as a health professional and become an effective servant of common grace.

You Are Not Alone: Help from the Past

The second-century North African apologist Tertullian defended the Christian faith against its detractors. In some of his written works, Tertullian was skeptical about the audacious claims of the Greeks of being the origin of all contemporary sciences and art. Tertullian argued that before the Greeks claimed to have developed medical arts, the Bible depicted faithful characters utilizing known medicines. Tertullian writes, "Let Aesculapius have been the first who sought and discovered cures: Isaiah mentions that he ordered Hezekiah medicine when he was sick. Paul, too, knows that a little wine does the stomach good."[2] Tertullian viewed the practice of medicine favorably and did not see a conflict between his belief that God can provide physical healing through a miracle or through the application of natural remedies. Tertullian himself had some training in medical science and used medical analogies in his apologetic works.[3]

In his writings Tertullian sometimes parallels medicine's application to the body with philosophy's application to the soul. The practice of medicine, he argues, is more disciplined than philosophy and provides more verifiable results. He says, "Moreover, I have looked into Medical Science also, the sister (as they say) of Philosophy, which claims as her function to cure the body, and thereby to have special acquaintance with the soul . . . while Medicine, on the other hand, has possessed the stringent demands of her art and practice."[4] Tertullian even prefers the practice

[2] Tertullian, *De Corona* (or *The Chaplet*), chap. 8 in *Ante-Nicene* Fathers, Vol. 3, p. 97.

[3] Timothy David Barnes, *Tertullian: A Historical and Literary Study* (Oxford: Clarendon Press, 1971), 205. Barnes notes that "curiosity" may have driven his interest in medicine.

[4] Tertullian, *De Anima* (or *A Treatise on the Soul*), chap. 2 in *Ante-Nicene Fathers*, Vol. 3, p.183.

of medicine because it does not make audacious claims for effectiveness with the body as philosophy does for the soul. Citing an ancient medical expert, Tertullian says that medicine has helped demonstrate the interconnectedness of the health of the body with a person's overall well-being. Tertullian explains, "Soranus, who is a most accomplished authority in medical science, affords us an answer, when he asserts that the soul is even nourished by corporeal aliments; that in fact it is, when failing and weak, actually refreshed oftentimes by food."[5] So as a CHP, your care for a person is holistic even though you may be treating only one aspect of the body. CHPs recognize the limits of their practice as well as their own personal limits; however, CHPs also serve others to bring God's grace to another person.

You Are Not Alone: Help from Above

As you are considering engaging your healthcare practice as a servant of God's grace, pray this prayer with us:

> *Lord, you are good and show your goodness throughout your creation. Would you help me to be an instrument of your goodness and grace in my healthcare setting? I need the power and guidance of your Word and the Holy Spirit to see my work as your work and pursue your will in each act of service. I pray, heavenly Father, that your will would be done in my healthcare setting and in my home as it is in heaven. In the name of Jesus, the Perfect Mediator. Amen.*

Reflection and Discussion Questions

1. Can you describe your professional journey? Can you describe your spiritual journey? Practice sharing the testimony of your journey

[5] *Treatise on the Soul*, Ch. 6.

with a trusted friend or colleague. Be sure to talk about how and when your professional and spiritual journeys converge.

2. Do you remember when you tried to keep your spiritual journey separate from your professional journey? With trusted friends or colleagues, discuss how you functioned at work and in life. What did you do to cope with the stress of serving on the front lines? How active or intentional were you about your relationship with God?
3. We provided a few examples from the Bible demonstrating the common grace of the Lord. There are quite a few more. Can you find others? For instance, grab your study Bible and read Ps 145:8–9 and Acts 14:16–17.
4. Can you describe your experiences with the practice behaviors we described as necessary for CHPs? What practices might you approach differently? If you are in a season where you are not practicing any of the behaviors (we get it . . . we've been there), start by reading a few verses from the Bible each day. John's Gospel is a good place to begin.
5. How would you describe your local church? How would you describe the preaching? How would you describe the teaching? How would you describe the congregation? Do you see evidence that the leaders of the church you attend live out what they preach and teach? If your church has a website, see if you can find a page or document that clearly states what they believe. If the church has a doctrinal statement, ask the pastor or an elder to go through and clearly explain each part of the statement.
6. Describe the relationship between grace and common grace. How are they different? How are they connected? Try explaining to a fellow believer what you do as a CHP through the lens of grace and common grace. See if you can explain things in a concise way, free of jargon, so that anyone can understand. Now, try explaining to a colleague, a friend, or a family member who you know does not have a relationship with Jesus Christ.

PART II

What Do You Do?

It is one thing to realize what you are as a health professional who believes in Jesus as Lord. It is another thing to figure out how to incorporate faith into your practice. Scripture is clear: God wants to come first in our lives. He wants firstfruits. He wants our relationship with the Son to be our identity. Not our primary identity, but our *entire* identity. For Christians in health care, the question is not, "How should we integrate our faith into our practice?" The question is, "How does our faith influence what we do in practice?" Just as our purpose as servants of common grace is revealed from within the narrative of Scripture, God provides guidance from his Word for serving patients effectively.

Biblical Practices from 2 Corinthians

The church in Corinth struggled with the pressures from their environment. They were surrounded by corruption and encouragement for partaking in just about every conceivable sin. They knew their faith in Jesus Christ freed them from the grips of sin, but the application of their faith remained a work in progress. Paul wrote 1 Corinthians to address their questions and take corrective action to reaffirm their commitment to the gospel. Upon receiving the letter, however, a few false teachers within the church questioned his authority and even slandered him. The context was set for 2 Corinthians.

Paul writes 2 Corinthians as a loving pastor. In an intensely personal and emotional plea, he reminds them of his integrity and that his only purpose is to pour out his life so that others may be perfected through Christ. Within the book he describes five biblical practices that every Christian should seek to embody. The five spiritual competencies are the key for serving patients effectively:

1. You provide comfort.
2. You forgive.
3. You point patients toward permanent glory.
4. You become a jar of clay.
5. You embrace your role as an ambassador of Christ.

The following chapters describe the application of the biblical practices in what CHPs do as servants of common grace. We then finish the book by offering strategies for thriving and enduring wherever you serve on the front lines in health care.

Chapter 4

Comfort

He comforts us in all our affliction, so that we may be able to comfort those who are in any kind of affliction, through the comfort we ourselves receive from God. —2 Cor 1:4

Ian Whitworth: Physician Assistant

Ian works in a large regional hospital as a physician assistant (PA). He practices as part of a team of five PA anesthesiologists where he provides support to the licensed anesthesiologist on duty. He is assigned to the pediatrics surgery center where he meets with patients and their families to record their medical history to ensure their safety when administering anesthesia. He also prepares patients for surgery and then monitors their conditions while they are under anesthesia. On a typical shift, Ian will see between twelve and eighteen patients.

Ian is married and has four children. He knows firsthand how unnerving it can be for parents watching their children being prepped for surgery. He remembers how helpless he felt when his youngest daughter was wheeled off for her tympanostomy (ear tubes) a few years ago. Although he knew she was having a very minor and typical procedure, it was still difficult to endure. When he meets with patients, he empathizes with how stressful his presence can be to everyone. Knowing how scary it can seem, he makes a point to comfort patients and their families by carefully explaining what they can expect. He also reassures parents by staying with them to answer any questions they have before moving onto the next child.

Emily Rose: Certified Nursing Assistant

Emily works in a long-term care facility where patients reside for a variety of reasons. For the last fifteen years, she has cared for patients nearing the end of life. The facility is likely their final earthly home. She spends most of her ten-hour shifts helping patients with direct health-care needs. She often turns or moves patients so they do not get bed sores. She helps them with grooming by brushing their hair, shaving them, and brushing their teeth. Some patients need help bathing and using the toilet. She will also help patients get dressed and ready if they need to travel. When she is away from patients, she is also responsible for stocking medical supplies and documenting all the care she provides. Usually, Emily loves caring for her patients and strives to put a smile on their faces. Even when the stress of her work seems overwhelming or she gets run down from helping with the mundane tasks of daily living, she finds joy in comforting patients who need her.

Providing comfort for patients may seem so basic for CHPs. Whenever people seek help from health professionals, there is an inherent expectation of receiving care that will alleviate their pain or ease their discomfort. Even when people go for wellness checks and routine exams, they are looking for comfort in knowing they are healthy. But where does the ability to comfort come from? What is the source of comfort? What about Ian? What role does comfort play in him being an effective PA anesthesiologist? Should he care less about empathizing with patients and families? How is Emily able to find joy after enduring fifteen years of taking care of others? What will sustain her for the years ahead? Will her training provide her with the inspiration to continue to comfort others? Will her salary sustain her desire to comfort others? Should she focus exclusively on her tasks? What about you? How do you prevent your practice with patients from becoming transactional? What is your source for providing comfort for patients seeking help? The answer is, we practice effectively as servants of common grace when we comfort others as an outpouring of comfort from God who comforts us in our afflictions.

Comfort Received from God

Paul describes the comfort received from God out of the depths of his own experience. When Paul met Jesus face-to-face on the road to Damascus, his purpose changed forever. He became the chosen instrument to share the gospel, experiencing immense suffering for the sake of the Messiah. But he did not face suffering alone. God came alongside him in the middle of all his afflictions to strengthen him with the courage needed to proclaim the message of the cross. Paul could describe God as the Father of mercies and of all comfort because he saw himself as needing the most mercy and the least deserving of comfort. Paul views himself as the worst of all sinners, saved by grace, and called as an example of the perfect loving patience of Jesus Christ so others would believe in him for eternal life (1 Tim 1:15–16).

In 2 Cor 1:3–7, Paul explains the link between comfort and affliction found in the infinite depths of God's mercy. After establishing his authority as an apostle and sharing a greeting of grace and peace from God the Father and the Lord Jesus Christ, he writes the following:

> Blessed be the God and Father of our Lord Jesus Christ, the Father of mercies and the God of all comfort. He comforts us in all our affliction, so that we may be able to comfort those who are in any kind of affliction, through the comfort we ourselves receive from God. For just as the sufferings of Christ overflow to us, so also through Christ our comfort overflows. If we are afflicted, it is

> for your comfort and salvation. If we are comforted, it is for your comfort, which produces in you patient endurance of the same sufferings that we suffer. And our hope for you is firm, because we know that as you share in the sufferings, so you will also share in the comfort.

Here Paul begins with an emotional exclamation praising God. His praise of God is personal, as he experienced so much suffering that he didn't think he had the strength to keep going. That's right, Paul felt as if he might not live much longer, and that would be a long-awaited relief. He was feeling worn down and saw no rescue in sight, or as he puts it, "completely overwhelmed—beyond our strength—so that we even despaired of life itself" (2 Cor 1:8).

Amid his transparent fears and failings, Paul explains the mathematics of how God's mercy worked in his life and works in the lives of all believers in Jesus Christ. As the trials and afflictions of the world abound, the comfort of God abounds even more. Where Paul suffered abundantly for serving Christ, through Christ he was comforted even more. But here is where the mercy and comfort of God multiply exponentially. God comforted Paul in his afflictions not simply to make his life easier. Oh no. God, the source of all comfort, comforted Paul so that Paul could comfort others in their afflictions, with the same comfort he received from God.

God's comfort for us works the same way. God takes our afflictions and turns them into a double blessing. He comforts us, brings us closer to him, and makes us rely less on ourselves and more on him, as the source of all comfort. But he comforts us for another purpose also—so that we may take the same comfort that transformed and saved our lives and share that comfort with other people in their afflictions. Stated differently, we comfort others in their distress with the only infinite source of comfort suitable for every situation.

The comfort Paul describes is different from how the world thinks of comfort. When most of us think of comfort, we likely think of actions taken to help ease or alleviate physical or mental pain. Sharing the comfort of God involves much more. The word "comfort" appears ten times in verses 3–7. The Greek word used for "comfort" connects to the image of someone coming alongside to help.

New Testament scholar Murray Harris explains this view of comfort for others' sake: "Paul's experience of God's support in the midst of *all* the tribulation he actually encountered . . . enabled him to become a channel for God's support to those who found themselves in *any type of* distress." Harris continues that Paul saw his suffering and comfort from God as helping his own spiritual life "but also as directly benefitting the fellow believers he ministered to."[1] A similar idea is portrayed in the Greek word Jesus used in John 14:16 for the Holy Spirit, which is often translated as "helper." The comfort Paul describes is that God literally stands at our side to help in whatever we are going through. He comes alongside to strengthen us, to encourage us, and to provoke in us the boldness to come alongside others in need of comfort. This is the kind of comfort that God calls CHPs, as his servants of common grace, to develop as a spiritual competency.

Spiritual Competency for Ourselves and Our Patients

We want you to experience joy on the front lines. We don't want you to burn out. There is such demand for health-care professionals, and we want you serving and persevering where there is so much opportunity to share the gospel with words and actions. We believe the only way you will thrive long-term is by giving deliberate attention to developing the spiritual competencies necessary to be effective with patients. But guess what? It is a reciprocal reinforcing process. The method for developing spiritual competencies with patients is by developing spiritual competencies

[1] Murray J. Harris, *The Second Epistle to the Corinthians: A Commentary on the Greek Text* (Grand Rapids: Eerdmans, 2005), 144. The italics in the Harris quotation are his.

within ourselves. And the method for developing spiritual competencies within ourselves is by developing spiritual competencies with patients. Stated differently, the extent to which you are active in developing your relationship with the Lord will directly influence your effectiveness as a servant of common grace. Let's explore what it means to develop comfort as a spiritual competency.

The key to accessing the comfort from God is found in 2 Cor 1:5–7. Paul says that the comfort we receive from God comes as we share abundantly in the sufferings of Christ. How are we "overflowing" in Christ's sufferings? Two things come to mind. First, Christ's sufferings occurred because *he was fully human*. In taking on a human nature to be like us, Christ opened himself to the human experience of suffering: hunger, loss, sickness, pain, temptation, torture, and death. As we suffer due to human frailties, our experience is like his suffering. It is important to experience this human suffering like Christ did, and we must suffer with the hope of resurrection. Jesus faced the reality of his own mistreatments, trial, and death, with the clear assurance that death would not consume him. To suffer in our human bodies, as sharing in his suffering, we must also have the active hope of our resurrection.

Second, and most importantly, *we have identified ourselves with Christ*. Paul was suffering because he boldly proclaimed Christ in hostile circumstances. When Paul spoke about Christ, many people believed and found new life in Christ and new community among God's people. However, many other people rejected the truths of Christ and treated Paul just as they had treated Christ himself. They wanted to kill him. Paul said that they had "despaired of life" and that they felt as if they "had received the sentence of death." Assuming that he was going to die for the cause of Christ, Paul said that he could not trust in his own abilities, his legal defense team, or his ability to diffuse a hostile crowd. Instead, this suffering caused Paul and his fellow workers not to trust in themselves "but in God who raised the dead." Paul is not just describing some abstract promise about God's character. He is saying, "If I die, God's got me." And he writes elsewhere, "For me, to live is Christ, and to die is gain" (Phil 1:21). Later in 2 Corinthians 1, Paul says that God strengthens him—and the Corinthian believers who suffer with him—in Christ. As a believer in Christ, you (like Paul) can trust in the deliverance that comes through Christ, even if that is in the ultimate deliverance of resurrection. In the meantime, we have the active hope in our suffering that is provided by the "paraclete" of the Holy Spirit who has been given to us "in our hearts as a down payment" of the promises to come (2 Cor 1:22).

Developing comfort as a spiritual competency happens as we pursue a life for Christ while also acknowledging the genuine afflictions we face. Wherever you are, take a minute and look at yourself in the mirror. What do you see? Can you see the permanent state of affliction you were destined to experience if you did not have a personal relationship with Jesus Christ? Can you claim the infinite mercies and comfort God gives you through the forgiveness of your sins, the Lord reaching across the chasm separating you from himself and transforming you into his son or daughter? What about the other afflictions you experienced or are experiencing? We encourage you to take inventory of all the times God comforted you amid the different physical, emotional, and social afflictions you endured through the years. Practice being deliberate in claiming and acknowledging the comfort you receive from God on an ongoing basis. Before each shift, think of how God has come alongside you in your life. Think of how he continues to comfort you. Embrace knowing that the Holy Spirit is with you always as a believer in Christ. Serve patients as a nurse, a doctor, a social worker, comforting them out of the outpouring of the comfort you receive from God. Based on our forty-plus years of combined experience (Michael and Angie), we expect that the more you practice being deliberate in coming alongside patients, the more situations you will encounter as opportunities to provide comfort. We also expect that as you stay consistent in God's Word and in prayer, those situations will reinforce your faithful dependence on the Lord and your purpose as a servant of common grace in health care.

Comfort for Different Occasions

Health-care settings are filled with opportunities to provide comfort. The sheer number of patients and colleagues needing comfort is overwhelming. Don't believe us? Try an experiment on your own. On your next shift, tune into the lives of every person you encounter at the hospital or clinic. See how long you can go before you feel inundated with opportunities to comfort. Check in with people at the front desk. Ask them how things are in their lives at home and at work. Next check in with colleagues as they are beginning and leaving their shifts. Now check in with every patient. What if we suggested checking in with every person sitting in the waiting room? Are you feeling overwhelmed yet? We are. Do you find yourself reaching the limits of your capacity to comfort? We do. The seemingly infinite number of people with their seemingly infinite number of needs is what Jesus refers to in Matt 9:36–38. Matthew writes:

> When he saw the crowds, he felt compassion for them, because they were distressed and dejected, like sheep without a shepherd. Then he said to his disciples, "The harvest is abundant, but the workers are few. Therefore, pray to the Lord of the harvest to send out workers into his harvest."

We can't meet all the needs in the vast harvest of our health-care settings. But here is what we *can* do. We *can* pray to the Lord of the harvest to send more CHPs into his harvest. We *can* trust God to be faithful in answering our prayers to provide the other laborers to meet the needs of others. We *can* rely on God to comfort us as we come alongside the patients and colleagues whom we *can* comfort in our sphere of influence. We *can* be strategic or discerning in looking for different ways to be effective when providing comfort. Below are four overlapping ways in which providing comfort might be helpful to patients and colleagues.

1. Comfort in Trouble

Look for opportunities to comfort in trouble. Take at face value Paul's words that God comforts us so that we can comfort patients and colleagues in *any* affliction. There is an invitation in God's Word here to expand the range of how we discern trouble. For almost every reason imaginable, patient and health professional interactions are inherently a disruption for patients. Their "status quo," or the routine of their lives, gets interrupted. Taking time to schedule appointments is a disruption. Rearranging work and life schedules to be able to show up for appointments is trouble. Completing all the paperwork, waiting to be seen, all the physical and mental health assessments and evaluations are trouble. Getting the medications patients need at the pharmacy and following the necessary treatment instructions is trouble. Paying for all of the health-care services, with or without insurance, is trouble.

Then there are all the troubles that come from the actual reasons patients seek help from CHPs in the first place. Patients seeking care usually experience enough disruption to their health and well-being to warrant them needing care. Whatever illness, injury, or concern patients bring with them, you should assume there are multiple compounding layers of troubles they are going through. We want you to expand your empathy for patient troubles so you can expand your opportunities to comfort them. Whatever your specific role is in health care, let your love for God and your love for people be evident in the comfort shared with patients. Let patients and colleagues see that for you health-care practice is never just transactional, an exchange of goods and services for a fee. Instead, demonstrate that health-care practice is your vocation whereby you are on mission to come alongside people in their troubles. Yes, you are there to treat patients with the training and expertise needed to provide the appropriate care. But you are also there to empathize with their troubles, minimize their disruptions, and relieve their worries.

2. Comfort in Suffering

Sometimes patients experience prolonged agony that gives rise to their worries. The physical or emotional pain just hurts so badly. Even if treatment can help, the suffering may not go away quickly enough. Patients may have to endure the pain. For some patients, the experience of such deep levels of suffering triggers lingering misery as they relive the pain over and over again. Of course, some patients will endure physical pain for the rest of their lives. My (Jason) father-in-law, Ronnie, was a bedridden, chronic pain patient for the last two decades of his life. He suffered day after day of pain, with hardly any relief. However, some days the most acute need was the need for comfort from the Lord, not just physical relief. Some patients will experience mental anguish for the rest of their lives. Then there are the families and friends of patients who suffer vicariously as they witness the misery of their loved ones, while they feel helpless to help them. Who can step in to endure the suffering with them? Can you?

In Genesis 16, Hagar, the Egyptian slave, was suffering. When Abraham and Sarah were in their eighties, Sarah began to believe that God was preventing her from bearing children. Instead of patiently waiting on the Lord, she took matters into her own hands, devising a plan to provide Abraham children. Hagar was the plan. Sarah gave Hagar to Abraham, who got her pregnant. Once Hagar was pregnant, Sarah became very upset. She began looking at Hagar with contempt and treating her very harshly—so harshly that Hagar decided to flee.

Hagar's suffering was prolonged and comprehensive. Can you empathize with her as you think about her circumstances? Here she is, a young, pregnant woman enslaved to a person who made her sleep with someone, got her pregnant, and then hated her for it. Sarah hated her so much that she created conditions bad enough to force this young woman to decide that it was safer to run away into the wilderness. Now Hagar was alone in the wilderness as a nobody. Her physical, emotional, and social suffering was not going away. Her fleeing perhaps made her even more vulnerable to continued suffering. Then, God showed up and comforted her. While Abraham and Sarah treated Hagar as an object they used as a means to an end, God called Hagar by her name.

God didn't take away Hagar's suffering. In fact, he had her return and submit to Sarah. What he did do for her was much more important. He spoke to her directly, he listened to her, he looked after her in her affliction, and he blessed her with a purpose. Hagar could return and endure the suffering because she understood she was not alone. She knew *El Ro'i* . . . the Hebrew word meaning "God who sees you."

Here is where a biblical understanding of your role in health care can tangibly inform your practice. Here is where God empowers you as his servant of common grace. Sure, you work alongside other health-care professionals to treat patients. Sure, you want patients to recover and get well. Sure, you want to relieve their pain. *But you are there for a bigger purpose.* You are there showing patients and colleagues amid their suffering that God is real, and he sees them. And you can comfort them in this way because you know yourself that God is real, and he sees you in your suffering. You have received comfort so that you can share that comfort with those in need.

3. Comfort in Distress

Comfort for patients can involve more than treating the specific issues that are causing trouble and suffering. As servants of common grace, we strive to care genuinely for the people we serve. This level of care means we are willing to be personally affected by and have concern for their overall well-being. Comfort then becomes all-encompassing, taking on the additional dimensions of comforting patients in their distress and comforting patients in their comfort. Why? Because God's love and comfort for us is comprehensive and all-consuming, and we want to share that kind of love at the front lines with patients and colleagues.

The need to comfort in distress usually emerges from some combination of two sources. In some instances, patients descend into prolonged discouragement as they experience the consequences of the decisions they made or actions they have taken. In other instances, patients experience prolonged distress after coping with difficult circumstances that seem to occur beyond their control. If you practice health care long enough, you will encounter the full spectrum of factors contributing to patients feeling distressed. As servants of common grace, to us the reason for their distress makes no difference; they present opportunities to comfort. The Bible is full of examples of comfort in distress. Here are just two of them.

In Genesis 50, Joseph's brothers had every reason to be distressed. They made a number of bad decisions that left them in a predicament where they were right to be concerned for their overall well-being. Their father Jacob had just died. They were grieving his loss. They now stood alone in a foreign country before their brother—the brother they mocked, abandoned, and sold into slavery. Sure, Joseph kept the peace while their father was still alive. But now their father was gone, and they were worried what Joseph might do to them. They were powerless to change their situation. What did Joseph do? He comforted them in their distress, provided for their tangible needs in a way that lifted their spirits, and transformed their view of the predicament. Read what he did for his brothers: "But Joseph said to them, 'Don't be afraid. Am I in the place of God? You planned evil against me; God planned it for good to bring about the present result—the survival of many people. Therefore don't be afraid. I will take care of you and your children.' And he comforted them and spoke kindly to them" (Gen 50:19–21).

In 1 Kings 19, Elijah also had every reason to be distressed. He finished confronting Ahab, perhaps the most wicked of all Israelite kings. Ahab abandoned the commandments of God and followed after the false god Baal. In an epic showdown against the false prophets of Baal, Elijah, a prophet of the living God, defeated the 450 false prophets. He then ordered all the Israelites who now believed in the living God to enact vengeance on all of the false prophets who had deceived them. When we get to chapter 19, it begins by Ahab sharing what happened with his maniacal pagan wife, Jezebel, who swore to kill Elijah.

Elijah was afraid. Moreover, even though he was faithful and obedient to following the Lord, he felt distressed and exhausted. It seemed he was tired of dealing with the animosity from the world. After walking all day into the wilderness, he sat down under a tree and told God that he had had enough. He then lay down under the tree and asked God to let him die. How do you think God responded? What do you think he did? He comforted Elijah by sending an angel to care for him. For two days the angel gently woke him up and had him eat food and drink water that God provided for him (in the middle of nowhere without access to food or water).

The love and care from the food and water lifted Elijah's spirits. He regained enough strength to make the long journey to Horeb, the mount of God. Once Elijah was at Horeb, God spoke to him. Although in his distress Elijah felt alone, scared, and threatened, God let him know that he was not the only one left. The Lord preserved a remnant of seven thousand in Israel who were also faithful. In other words, God transformed Elijah's view of the situation. The Lord then sent Elijah off on two additional missions, before having him anoint Elisha, his successor.

Elijah experienced circumstances affecting his well-being that were quite different from Joseph's brothers. He was distressed by consequences beyond his control that occurred because of his faithfulness to the Lord. Nevertheless, because God is the Father of all mercies and all comfort, he comforted Elijah and Joseph's brothers with the same grace and love. He spoke kindly to them in their distress, met tangible needs in a way that lifted their spirits, and transformed their view of their predicament. You can do the same for patients and colleagues as a servant of common grace.

Recognize that your patients and colleagues are likely coping with life stressors affecting their well-being. Things might become so overwhelming that they fall subject to feeling dejected, downcast, and gloomy about their lives. Or they may feel so grief-stricken that they live with a sense of hopelessness and sadness. In these situations, provide comfort targeting their overall state of being. Serve patients and colleagues as a servant of common grace by coming alongside them in their seemingly permanent state of misery, temporarily lift their spirits by meeting their tangible needs, and point them toward the source of all comfort who has the power to transform their view of their predicament. When you do, you will experience the joy of helping many patients move from feeling distressed to feeling a sense of comfort.

4. Comfort in Comfort

Seek to comfort patients and colleagues in their comfort. Remember, comfort for us as CHPs is more than worldly actions focused on easing pain. It is a willingness and desire to stand alongside people in whatever they are going through—good or bad. God uses CHPs in a unique way. We get to engage people at their lowest moments of suffering and distress. We get to participate in their healing. Then we get to interact with them when they are well (at least from a temporary, worldly perspective), giving them guidance for continued healing and wellness. When we comfort in comfort, we are perhaps most aligned in our roles as servants of common grace. We are also demonstrating our distinctiveness from other health professionals. The reason being that we at once share in the joyful celebration of the temporary restoration of patients, remember what they have been through, and point them to the need to experience permanent restoration.

Can you think of a time when you, or someone you know, had to go to the doctor after suffering an injury? I (Michael) remember several years ago playing kickball with several different families in the neighborhood. It was my turn to kick. An eight-year-old kid from next door rolled the ball. As I had done many times before, I took my steps, kicked the ball, and ran to first base as fast as I could. Only on this occasion, as soon as I took off for first base, I felt as if someone had shot me with a pistol in my right calf. After hopping on one leg to the base (couldn't let my team down), I looked down and saw my right leg swollen like a balloon. In haste two friends helped me hobble to the car and my wife took me straight to the emergency room.

It turned out my gastrocnemius snapped when I attempted to run to the base. The doctor in the ER put me in a boot, prescribed medication to help with the pain, and then referred me to an orthopedist. The following week, with my leg stabilized and the pain subsided, my visit with the orthopedist was more comfortable. The doctor comforted me in my discomfort as we laughed at how silly it was that I hurt my leg playing kickball. She assured me that my leg was healing properly and that I was going to be relatively okay. She cautioned me to be patient with myself as the leg continued healing over the next few weeks. But she also told me things would be different as I lost the use of that muscle. Even today, every time I look down, I see a giant depression in the back of my right leg reminding me that things will never be the same. As servants of common grace, you should seek to do likewise: remind patients that even as you celebrate their improved health, things will never be permanently better. Only belief in Jesus Christ can make that happen. He is the exemplar for comforting in comfort. Let's look at one example.

The Last Supper (The Passover Seder Transformed)

Jesus Christ teaches us how to comfort in comfort through his participation in and transformation of the Last Supper. The Last Supper is a Passover seder celebrated in comfort to remember temporary deliverance from distress, transformed by Jesus into a remembrance of permanent deliverance for those who believe in him as Lord and Savior. The celebration of Passover is in remembrance of the time in Israel's history when the angel of the Lord moved through Egypt destroying the firstborn of all people and animals (see Exodus 11 and 12). This was the final of the ten signs or "plagues" God visited upon Egypt designed to force Pharaoh to let the Israelites leave the country and their captivity. The Israelites were commanded by God to take the blood of a male lamb—one without blemish—and smear it on the doorposts of their houses, and then eat the rest of the flesh in haste, because it is the Lord's Passover. When the angel of the Lord saw the blood, he would *PASS OVER* that house.

At the Last Supper, Jesus celebrates the Passover with his disciples in comfort. Luke 22:14 states, "When the hour came, he reclined at the table, and the apostles with him." Whereas the Israelites ate their meal with their belts fastened, their sandals on, and their staffs in their hands, the Passover celebration is eaten in comfort, remembering what God did to free his people. Jesus comes alongside his disciples as comfort to remember their temporary deliverance. But as he comforted them, he pointed the way toward permanent deliverance. It was as comfort that he transformed the ceremonial handwashing into the washing of their feet (see John 13:1–20). It was as comfort that he transformed the meaning of the bread and the meaning of the wine (see Luke 22:19–20). Jesus, the perfect Lamb of God, comforted in comfort while knowing it was his blood that would cause God's judgment to pass over eternally all those who believe in him, guaranteeing their salvation.

As believers, we are invited to the table for communion with our Lord, the Comforter. We are a part of a community of faith that has placed our hope in Jesus as our rescue from the captivity of our sin and its consequences, including suffering. We take comfort in his suffering, remembered in the Supper, which allows us to have joy during struggles, patience during trials, and hope in suffering. As we pass the bread and cup to others in our church family, we rehearse the truth that our comfort is to be shared with other sufferers so that we may rejoice together in Christ (for eternity). As Paul writes, "And our hope for you is firm, because we know that as you share in the sufferings, so you will also share in the comfort" (2 Cor 1:7).

Conduit of Comfort and Evidence

Focusing on the spiritual competency of comfort can radically alter everything about your work. Sure, there will always be stressful, seemingly unbearable aspects of your profession. The combination of attending to patients while working long hours, being on call, completing all the necessary paperwork, and dealing with insurance companies, pharmacies, and other providers can divert your attention away from why you are there. If you focus too much or too long on all the things that make serving patients difficult, it could steal your joy.

We (Michael and Angie) have seen it. Both of us know colleagues who burned out because they lost sight of their objective. Burnout does not have to happen to you. You have a purpose in health care that transcends the normal and mundane. Focus on providing comfort throughout your day and you will, in part, fulfill that purpose. When you look for opportunities to give comfort, you align your heart, your mind, and your actions as a CHP with God's purpose for putting you on the front lines. You essentially become a conduit of comfort and a conduit of evidence. Let us explain. The whole interaction between you and your patients is but a foretaste of the interactions between both of you and the Lord that have eternal significance. Regardless of the beliefs of your patients, comfort for them comes from the unearned abundance of perfect comfort you receive from the Lord. In turn, the comfort provided serves as evidence for you and your patients that God is real and that he comforts. Your transfer of comfort to patients stems from love for others that is grounded in your own faith in God and your wholehearted love for him. You display God's love for his creatures in ways that are tangible even for those who have not yet believed. Ultimately, you get to reinforce God's steadfast love for Christian patients, while pointing non-believers to the only One who can guarantee eternal salvation.

You won't always comfort others well. At some point you will work with patients you don't like very much. Your personal life may at times cause your own distress that interferes with your health-care practice. You may suffer your own physical and mental health issues where you need comfort from other CHPs and from your church family. As a pastor, I (Jason) realize that Sunday worship gatherings and small group discipleship are vital places for hurting CHPs to be rejuvenated in the gospel so that they can be comfort-givers (not just "caregivers") again. When you fall short, which you will, forgiveness is the way forward. Forgiving ourselves and forgiving others is the best way to get back to providing comfort. In fact, practicing comfort and practicing forgiveness go hand-in-hand. As much as we encourage you to look for opportunities to comfort others, we encourage you to be ready to forgive. That is why forgiveness is the next spiritual competency we emphasize in the following chapter.

You Are Not Alone: Help from the Past

In his work *Confessions*, St. Augustine, a fifth-century pastor in North Africa, describes how he came to trust in the Lord. It was not an easy journey for him. He had pursued his own self-centered life and had little time to consider the Christian faith that had been shared with him by his faithful mother, Monica. At an early age, Augustine heard the gospel, but he would not yet submit to its truth. He pursued other things in life and thought contentment would only come through selfish indulgences and career success.

As Augustine was pursuing his career advancement, two things happened to him that pushed him further into despair: a severe sickness that almost took his life and a disillusionment with some of the secular "truths" that he had trusted in. After decades of praying for him, Monica finally saw God's work in Augustine's life bring him to faith.

Augustine was exposed to the preaching of the bishop of Milan, Ambrose. The preacher's sermons were stylistic in craft and persuasive in content. However, it was not a particular sermon that convinced Augustine, but it was God's consistent calling to him when he had hit "the bottom" of life. In *Confessions*, Augustine describes this crucial season:

> To you, fount of mercies, she redoubled her petitions and tears, begging that you would hasten your help (Ps. 69:1), and lighten my darkness (Ps. 17:29). She would zealously run to the Church to hang on Ambrose's lips, to "the fount of water bubbling up to eternal life" (Jn. 4:14). She loved that man as an angel of God

> (Gal. 4:14), when she knew that it was through him that I had been brought to that state of hesitancy and wavering. I was to pass through that sickness to health, but with a more acute danger intervening, like that high fever preceding recovery which the physicians call "the critical onset."[2]

Augustine's troubles had led him to the comfort of the Scriptures. He and his friend, Alypius, had come to the end of their spiritual searching. Augustine read the Scriptures, found the mercy of God, sought out his friend, and the two of them shared their good news with Monica. In *Confessions*, Augustine describes the moment that he found his comfort in God himself when in his tears he turned to Rom 13:13–14:

> There I had put down the book of the apostle when I got up. I seized it, opened it and in silence read the first passage on which my eyes lit: "Not in riots and drunken parties, not in eroticism and indecencies, not in strife and rivalry, but put on the Lord Jesus Christ and make no provision for the flesh in its lusts" (Rom. 13:13–14). I neither wished nor needed to read further. At once, with the last words of this sentence, it was as if a light of relief from all anxiety flooded into my heart. All the shadows of doubt were dispelled.
>
> (30) Then I inserted my finger or some other mark in the book and closed it. With a face now at peace I told everything to Alypius. . . . Without any agony of hesitation, he joined me in making a good resolution and affirmation of intention, entirely congruent with his moral principles in which he had long been greatly superior to me. From there we went to my mother and told her. She was filled with joy. We told her how it had happened. She exulted, feeling it to be a triumph, and blessed you who "are powerful to do more than we ask or think" (Eph. 3:20). She saw that

---

[2] Saint Augustine, *Confessions*, trans. Henry Chadwick in Oxford World's Classics (New York: Oxford University Press, 2008), 91 (Book 6, Chapter 1).

> you had granted her far more than she had long been praying for in her unhappy and tearful groans. The effect of your converting me to yourself . . .[3]

Your persistent prayers and your providing comfort (in word and deed) to those who are suffering could be the means that the Lord uses to bring your patient or coworker to the eternal healing and comfort found in the gospel. Just as Monica rejoiced in the salvation of her son Augustine, you too could rejoice at someone finding their comfort in God.

You Are Not Alone: Help from Above

As you are recognizing the challenges and joys of bringing God's comfort to places of suffering, pray this prayer with us:

> *Lord, you are the God who comforts. Would you help me to be an instrument of your comfort in my health-care setting? I need to receive your comfort in my own troubles and not look to temporary and unsatisfying reliefs. I ask for the help of the Comforter, the Holy Spirit, to see my work as your means of comfort to others. I pray, heavenly Father, that you would give me the "daily bread" of strength, patience, and focus I need to comfort and serve others today. In the name of Jesus, the Bread of Life. Amen.*

Reflection and Discussion Questions

1. Think back to a time when you were dealing with physical, emotional, social, and/or spiritual affliction. In a small group, can you share about what was causing the affliction? As you think back, can you share what brought you comfort?

---

[3] Augustine, *Confessions*, 153 (Book 8, Chapter 12).

2. If you were presenting a workshop comparing how comfort is understood in the world and how comfort is understood in the Bible, how would you explain the differences?
3. Incorporate a desire to comfort into your prayer life. Begin asking God in prayer before each shift to put you in situations to provide comfort. Be deliberate to take a few minutes after each shift (perhaps when you first get to your car or get on the bus or subway to go home) to thank the Lord for comforting you as you sought to comfort others that day.
4. We only touched upon a few examples in Scripture demonstrating that God is the God of all comfort. Take some time to examine other examples. For instance, read about David and Mephibosheth (2 Samuel 9) and read the parable of the Good Samaritan (Luke 10:25–37). What stirred David and the Good Samaritan to take the opportunity to comfort?
5. At the end of the chapter, we describe comfort as a form of evidence that confirms God is real. Can you describe situations in your life where you experienced evidence that confirmed God is real? What role did comfort (giving, receiving, or experiencing comfort) play as part of the situation?

Chapter 5

Forgiveness

As a result, you should instead forgive and comfort him. Otherwise, he may be overwhelmed by excessive grief. —2 Cor 2:7

Adilynn "Adi" Beeman: A Physician Assistant

Adi provides primary care in an integrated behavioral health-care setting. Adi embraces this population as mental health patients experience significant medical issues but often have limited access to health-care delivery. Nearly twenty years of primary care experience in a variety of settings has prepared Adi well for this holistic, integrated care model. Adi looks forward to collaborating with her psychiatric CHP colleagues to continuously coordinate optimal patient care approaches.

Frank Wood, one of Adi's most challenging patients, has been dealing with schizophrenia for over forty years, as his first psychotic episode was documented to have occurred around thirteen years of age. Medically, Frank has hypertension, hyperlipidemia, and prediabetes. Mentally, Frank is continually tortured by auditory hallucinations, "voices" telling him how bad he is. Frank ruminates on pervasive thoughts focused on a life of condemnation. He exhibits extreme paranoia that surrounds every thought, action, and behavior, believing everything he does or thinks about is being judged as a sin and fearing eternity in hell.

Medically, Frank's blood pressure is normotensive, well controlled by antihypertensive therapy, and his blood work demonstrates statin therapy success. Frank has also joined Adi's walking group, reflecting a substantial increase in his physical activity, yet the antipsychotics are still not working to relieve him of pervasive negative thoughts and hallucinations.

During a routine physical checkup, Adi began asking some questions regarding Frank's childhood. Much to her surprise, she learned that Frank's dad was an ordained pastor who devoted his life to serving God and shepherding the lost. Frank spoke of his father with great respect and then suddenly broke out into tears. Frank shared how his father lived a double life of serving Christ by day and being an alcoholic by night. Frank's father would preach like none other, then "closet drink" at a local neighborhood bar. Frank shared how his dad would come home hammered and then physically abuse Frank and his little sister. In a drunken stupor, as he was striking them with his belt he would say, "I'm going to beat the devil out of you." Frank shared his understanding of this abuse as his father's way of ensuring that Frank and his sister would not end up spending eternity in hell.

Adi was awestruck, and she shared this finding at the next team meeting. Adi and the psychiatrist quickly surmised that Frank needed more than antipsychotics to work through years of childhood abuse. He needed a professional to help him process his past so that he could function better in the future. The antipsychotics alone will only continue to numb his pain and mask his issues. This situation was ultimately calling for forgiveness, only true forgiveness afforded by the saving grace of Jesus Christ.

Corey Russell: A Physical Therapist

Corey is a Doctor of Physical Therapy (DPT) providing care in an inpatient rehabilitation facility. Most of his patients come to the facility after experiencing significant trauma that resulted in life-threatening and life-altering injuries. Corey's work is time intensive as well as mentally and physically demanding. It involves conducting initial comprehensive assessments, reviewing patients' medical histories, and then developing individualized treatment plans. The treatment he provides is hands-on, using exercises, stretching, and equipment to help patients regain their range of motion, manage their pain, and improve their quality of life in the least restrictive and most life-normative environment possible. The recovery process for his patients will take weeks, months, and sometimes years. During that time, Corey must carefully record patients' progress and modify their treatment plans as needed. He also must educate patients and their family members about the recovery plans and set clear goals and expected outcomes.

Corey began working with Jeff Tanner seven months ago. Shortly after his fifteenth birthday, Jeff and his mother were driving home after his baseball practice when she ran a red light, and they were T-boned by a pickup truck. The truck smashed flush into the passenger front seat where Jeff was sitting. Though his mother escaped with mild bruises and abrasions, the impact from the truck left Jeff with sixty-two bone fractures and significant blood loss from multiple lacerations and puncture wounds. After being airlifted to the hospital, surviving eleven hours of surgery, and three weeks of a medically induced coma, Jeff regained consciousness. A few days later the lead physician referred him to the facility for long-term rehabilitation treatment.

Jeff started as a difficult patient. Corey needed to develop a treatment intervention plan to assist Jeff with just about every task. He was dependent on staff for sitting up, eating, drinking, bathing, using the toilet. Additionally, though he had feeling in his lower extremities, he was temporarily paralyzed from the waist down. Mentally, Jeff oscillated back and forth between being withdrawn and enraged. For the first few weeks he was awful to be around. Every treatment session ended with Jeff in a crying fit, hurling insults at Corey and the support staff. As time went on, however, Jeff started making progress. He regained some strength and mobility, could stand on his own, and could walk with assistance. On his last day in the facility, he hugged Corey, full of joy, thanking him for everything. He also told Corey that he plans to pursue physical therapy in college after he graduates high school.

In his twelve years of working at the facility, Corey is used to working with patients like Jeff Tanner—patients who are at their worst. Their progress is often slow and arduous, causing them to get frustrated. They get frustrated as they grieve the loss of their former selves and adapt to their "new normal." In their frustration, patients can get angry, act out of character, and say hurtful things they don't mean. Patients and family members have yelled at him, cursed at him, cried to him, and shared their worst fears with him. Corey does his best to communicate empathy and to not take things too personally. Whether people are cordial or unpleasant to be around, he realizes that he must continue returning each day to work with them so they can recover well enough to leave the facility someday. Corey knows from experience that what they need from him most is patience, forgiveness, and love.

Forgiveness from the Consequences of Sin

Patient care brings CHPs face-to-face with the consequences of sin. Physical illness, mental illness, and death are repercussions of the fall of humanity. In some instances, patients make poor decisions and bad judgments that worsen their situations. In other instances, patients become ill because of their family heredity or are injured due to the actions of others. Regardless of the specific circumstances, CHPs will often engage people when the consequences of sin are laid bare for others to see. As Adi seeks to provide Frank Woods the best care, she learns of his history as a victim of verbal and physical abuse. She understands the abuse for what it is—a shroud of darkness, influencing his long-term health. Adi treats his symptoms with antipsychotic medication, but the hurt and pain contributing to his issues will need something more for Frank to find healing. Likewise, Corey developed an effective plan using the appropriate treatments to help Jeff Tanner learn to function again and manage his pain. But Jeff Tanner needs something more to experience healing. Adi and Corey recognize the influential role of forgiveness in the overall well-being of both patients. Without forgiveness, the grief, the hurt, the anger, and the frustrations experienced from the tangible consequences of sin will be too much to bear.

Here we set forth an obvious but profound statement that can transform how you view your practice as a CHP: *health-care practice is caring for patients who have grieved others and have been grieved by others, and it is done by CHPs who have grieved others and have been grieved by others.* Let us explain. All patients seeking our care have their own history of sin. At one point or another every patient has done things to other people that caused hurt and pain. When we treat patients on the front lines, we are confronted with our own history of sins, times when we have been hurt or have caused hurt. As a CHP, you are going to work with patients who remind you of people you have hurt. You will also work with patients who remind you of people who have hurt you. What you do with the grief and hurt you have experienced and caused will go a long way in shaping the effectiveness of your practice. If you try to ignore or compartmentalize the role of grief and hurt, you will miss out on opportunities to share the gospel through patient care. God makes it clear in his Word what he wants us to do with the grief and hurt we have caused and experienced. He wants us pointing the way to Jesus through our words and actions by practicing forgiveness out of an outpouring of our love for him who he sent to forgive.

Forgiveness from Love

Paul emphasizes the critical role of forgiveness in 2 Corinthians 2. After describing the God of all comfort in chapter 1, he uses the rest of that chapter to explain why he changed his plans, deciding to hold off on visiting them again. Paul explained that he was concerned about causing more pain and experiencing more pain. He loved the people of that church so much that he felt such a burden after he had to address some of the flagrant sins that were being permitted in the church (see 1 Corinthians 1–6). At the beginning of chapter 2, he makes it clear that he did not want to cause or feel any more pain toward them. What he cared most about was communicating the abundant love he had for them. Paul demonstrated the practice of forgiveness toward the church in Corinth, then writes the powerful words about the importance of forgiveness in the following verses. He writes in 2 Cor 2:5–11:

> If anyone has caused pain, he has caused pain not so much to me but to some degree—not to exaggerate—to all of you. This punishment by the majority is sufficient for that person. As a result, you should instead forgive and comfort him. Otherwise, he may be overwhelmed by excessive grief. Therefore I urge you to reaffirm your love to him. I wrote for this purpose: to test your character to see if you are obedient in everything. Anyone you forgive, I do too. For what I have forgiven—if I have forgiven anything—it is for your benefit in the presence of Christ, so that we may not be taken advantage of by Satan. For we are not ignorant of his schemes.

The sharing of the gospel was too important for Paul to allow room for personal resentments and pain to fester. The context of his heartfelt plea to forgive comes after he admonished the church to dismiss a man who was engaging in such perverse sexual immorality that his behaviors would not even be tolerated among pagans. The dismissal, however, was not enforced out of hatred or anger at the person. Rather, it was encouraged out of an obedient love for Jesus Christ. He hoped that this man would experience the worldly consequences of his sin, bringing him to a place of sorrow, and eventually to repentance. Paul shared in verses 5 and 6 that enough is enough. Whatever grief this man caused, it was time for the church to move forward. It was now important for the church to turn their attention to forgiveness and love to bring about restoration. The consequences for remaining upset were too severe for everyone involved. As he demonstrated in his letter, Paul makes it clear that he has forgiven this man on their behalf as a demonstration of his love.

Forgiveness coming from a demonstration of love is similar for CHPs practicing forgiveness in medical settings—the primary difference being that patients always present us with observable consequences of sin. When patients attend church (believers and non-believers), they can pretend or perform in front of others so that church leaders and laypeople have no idea what burdens they are carrying or have caused. Competent CHPs see in specific ways the scars and burdens patients bring to us, and their information is normally documented in their medical files. Whether patients are believers or non-believers, the principle of restoration through forgiveness and love is equally important for providing effective care. Moreover, the reasons for which Paul encourages forgiveness can influence the prognosis of patient outcomes and their overall well-being. It can also be, along with comfort, the most effective practice for sharing the gospel with patients through our words and actions.

Reasons for Practicing Forgiveness

Paul implicitly and explicitly infers five reasons for practicing forgiveness. Each of the reasons makes forgiveness important. Taken together, practicing forgiveness is vital for you to be an effective servant of common grace. Practicing forgiveness, which is rooted in Christ's forgiveness, allows you to avoid extending relational strains; to reaffirm your love for others (based on God's love for you and them); to remain obedient to the one who sends you to the front line; to transcend grief and hurt with radical love and discipleship; to thwart Satan who hopes to outwit us by causing division, chaos, and hurt feelings.

Forgive to Avoid Extending Relational Strain

As the old saying expresses it, "Forgiveness is a two-way street." Another spin on this idea is that there are two people who benefit from forgiveness: those who receive it and those who give it. In 2 Cor 2:7, Paul says that the one who needs to be forgiven can be "overwhelmed by excessive grief" if he does not receive forgiveness from the other members of his faith family. While this man had deserved discipline (and relational separation), the call now was to restore him to fellowship with the body and caring relationships. As one NT scholar puts it, "It is the corporate responsibility of the church to punish wrongdoing (2 Cor 2:6; 10:6), to excommunicate in the case of persistent sin (1 Cor 5:2, 10–13), and to reinstate the repentant (2 Cor 2:7–8)."[1] Forgiveness restores relationships that have been broken by sinful actions and sinful attitudes.

There is just too much going on at the front lines in health care for CHPs to carry strained relationships into practice. Come to work repressing hurt feelings and you will be distracted, withdrawn, and less patient when you provide care. You will also be a burden to colleagues working on your shift. Continue remaining upset and you will burn out or engage in destructive behavior that could get you fired. Paul encourages us to extend the same forgiveness that we have received from Christ to others who have wronged us (Col 3:13). Forgiveness restores relationships and restores our peace. We can avoid becoming overwhelmed by strained relationships by seeking to forgive and comfort. Unless you live your life in a vacuum chamber, you are going to do things that cause others grief, even family and friends. You will also experience being on the receiving end of words and actions that cause you grief. It is important to practice forgiving others (and yourself) so that you will be free to focus on serving patients who need forgiveness.

---

[1] Linda L. Belleville, *2 Corinthians*, IVPNTC 8 (Downers Grove: InterVarsity, 1996), 74.

Frank Wood and Jeff Tanner illustrate the consequences of carrying around excessive sorrow. Although it is impossible to determine the exact reasons Frank was diagnosed with schizophrenia, it seems his quality of life was influenced by the burdens he carried from the hurt done to him as a child. He has spent *forty years* taking psychotic medications. The negative auditory hallucinations, the pervasive thoughts on condemnation, and his extreme paranoia, at a minimum, are connected to his verbal and physical abuse. Who knows what his prognosis would have been if he had trusted someone enough to share what had happened; perhaps a CHP tuned into his need for forgiveness. It seems reasonable to conclude that excessive sorrow contributed to nearly a lifetime of physical and mental health issues. The good news is that Adi recognizes the limits of the medications to treat his symptoms. As a CHP, she allows herself to view the situation from an eternal perspective. She can now refer Frank for treatment with someone who can help him forgive and find comfort from God who comforts us in all our afflictions.

Jeff Tanner experienced the burden of excessive sorrow after his accident. One minute he is joyfully heading home as a seemingly carefree teenager from baseball practice, the next minute he is trapped at an inpatient facility in his broken body. His mother was probably burdened from excessive hurt as well. Though their feelings were understandable, they probably didn't help his rehabilitation. Corey was on the receiving end of Jeff's grief at the beginning of his treatment. Based on where he worked, he likely was on the receiving end of grief from a lot of different patients. Instead of harboring resentment or taking things personally, Corey returned to work with Jeff each day until he recovered well enough to leave the facility. His willingness to practice forgiveness and comfort gave Jeff the space he needed to begin restoring his life again. He and his mother will need to continue forgiving and comforting each other as they live into their new normal. They will need to reaffirm their love for each other, just as Corey reaffirmed his love for them as a CHP, treating them as he does all patients—as fellow humans made in God's image and likeness.

Forgive to Reaffirm Your Love for Others

Practicing forgiveness to avoid extended relational strain and excessive sorrow on its own is not enough. Health professionals who do not believe in Jesus as Lord and Savior can probably incorporate that basic level of forgiveness with patients. The rationale is that avoiding strain and sorrow can be a part of overall patient care that might help with outcomes. In essence, forgiveness in this instance can be a means to an end. The other reasons for forgiveness require a transcendental view of health-care practice that views people as more than finite living organisms.

One of the things that sets you apart from your colleagues is that you are there practicing medicine representing the love and character of God. David succinctly describes God when he writes, "For you, Lord, are kind and ready to forgive, abounding in faithful love to all who call on you" (Ps 86:5). Now you are not always going to feel as if you are full of patience, forgiveness, and love. There will be days when your personal and professional life just get entangled and overwhelmed. Different people will upset you and you will upset them. Additionally, as we addressed in the last chapter, you as a limited, fallen, finite being are unable to comfort all your patients and all your colleagues in all their afflictions. But here is what you can do as a CHP. You can seek to align your heart intentionally with God by practicing forgiveness regularly so that you can reaffirm the love you have for others (and even yourself) as God's creatures. Notice the connection the apostle Paul makes between human forgiveness and divine forgiveness as well as human love and divine love. Ephesians 4:32 says, "And be kind and compassionate to one another, forgiving one another, just as God also forgave you in Christ." Then, two verses later (5:2), Paul writes, "and walk in love, as Christ also loved us and gave himself for us."

When you see patients, you are there representing God (and his love) on the front lines working with people calling upon you for help. If you want to be effective as a CHP, it is imperative that you come to work knowing who you really are. You are a redeemed child of God who was a broken sinner deserving of judgment and death whose sins have been forgiven. You are a redeemed child of God living under no condemnation because you are in Christ Jesus (Rom 8:1). You are a redeemed child of God who, through Jesus Christ, is known personally and has a specific, permanent place waiting for you in heaven with the Lord (John 14:2). God first loved you, while you were still a sinner (Rom 5:8). When you hold on to hurts, mistakes, or disappointments, you risk clouding out your identity as a child of God. Even worse, you risk becoming so self-absorbed in your pain that you can get distracted from why God has you serving him in the first place.

Make it a priority to spend time in confessional prayer with God each day. Bring all your hurts, grievances, and shortcomings to him. Leave all that baggage where it belongs, with Christ Jesus. Have enough faith in Jesus to forgive yourself, then move on. Keep yourself free from bearing the weight of self-condemnation. It is a weight you are not meant to carry. Instead, come to work ready to practice health care looking for opportunities to reaffirm the God-inspired love you have for your patients and your colleagues.

Forgive to Remain Obedient to the Lord

Paul makes it clear that practicing forgiveness is a test of obedience. Strip away whatever emotions emerge when we have grieved others or have been grieved by others. Opportunities to practice forgiveness ultimately become the deepest assessments of the ownership or allegiance of our souls. He writes in Rom 6:16–18:

> Don't you know that if you offer yourselves to someone as obedient slaves, you are slaves of that one you obey—either of sin leading to death or of obedience leading to righteousness? But thank God that, although you used to be slaves of sin, you obeyed from the heart that pattern of teaching to which you were handed over, and having been set free from sin, you became enslaved to righteousness.

Is your health-care practice about you or about God? If we asked your colleagues to describe how they can tell your love for your patients and colleagues comes from serving the Lord as a servant of common grace at the hospital or clinic, what would they share? Are you fulfilling your vocation as a CHP counting everything as rubbish because of the surpassing worth of knowing Jesus Christ as Lord (Phil 3:7–8)? If you allow mistakes, shortcomings, disappointments, disagreements, or disputes to take root and fester, you will become miserable. All the stresses of serving on the front lines will overwhelm you. The love and care for your patients and colleagues will suffer as you will focus too much on yourself.

The opposite will happen if you practice forgiveness regularly. When you practice forgiveness, you release yourself from the burdens of disdain and resentment by bringing your complaints to the cross. As Paul would state it, you are no longer a slave to your flesh, but to God's righteousness. You are then free to focus less on yourself and more on obedience to whom you belong. Sometimes, the command to forgive others seems impossible to obey. Some people are difficult to forgive, and moving on from offenses seems to make light of them. The truth of the gospel recognizes the magnitude of offenses (including ours against God) while acknowledging undeserved and unreserved forgiveness as the right application of Christ's death for sin. Practice forgiveness to remain obedient to the Lord and he will be faithful to produce the fruit (or provide the evidence) that makes you an effective servant of common grace. Patients and colleagues will see the difference.

Forgiveness Rooted in Christ

Just what kind of fruit will patients and colleagues see? They will see a joy and a purpose in serving as a CHP. The joy will be unmistakable because it is rooted in a genuine relationship with Jesus Christ. They will see that you have responded to Christ's lavish forgiveness of your sins with extending that loving forgiveness to others. When you confessed your sins, repented, and believed in your heart that Jesus is Lord, it changed everything about your life. Paul writes in Gal 2:20, "I have been crucified with Christ, and I no longer live, but Christ lives in me. The life I now live in the body, I live by faith in the Son of God, who loved me and gave himself for me." And in Col 2:13–14, he writes, "And when you were dead in trespasses and in the uncircumcision of your flesh, he made you alive with him and forgave us all our trespasses. He erased the certificate of debt, with its obligations, that was against us and opposed to us, and has taken it away by nailing it to the cross."

Jesus canceled the record of any debts that stood against you. The life you live in the flesh you now live by faith in Christ, knowing that though deserving of death, Christ bore the penalty of all your sins. Though Jesus did nothing wrong, he loved you so much that he laid down his life for you so God the Father would forgive you of your sins forever, and you would have eternal life. Made alive in Christ, he invites you to become his disciple by denying yourself, picking up your cross daily, and following him.

Practicing forgiveness rooted in Christ gives you a unique perspective for approaching health care.

As his disciple, thrive as a CHP by practicing forgiveness rooted in Christ. Christ healed you from your position of death, grief, and separation from God with radical love and radical forgiveness. If you are deliberate to embrace the complete transformation, it will help make you an effective servant of common grace. Practicing forgiveness rooted in Christ gives you a unique perspective for approaching health care. You, who once deserved justice and condemnation for all the wrongs you ever committed and will ever commit, have received infinite mercy and grace. Whatever patients, colleagues, or health-care administrators throw at you on the front lines, your relationship with Jesus frees you from worrying about yourself in practice. Trust Jesus to be concerned for your well-being; instead, use your freedom looking for opportunities to share mercy and grace.

Corey trusted Jesus to be concerned for his well-being. When patients like Jeff Tanner are unkind or angry, he demonstrates grace and mercy in how he returns to work with them. He seems less concerned about himself and more concerned about caring for patients. Sure, Corey will have days or shifts where things get to him more than usual. But when that happens, he can practice forgiving himself and forgiving others, knowing that his life, his identity, and his role as a CHP are secure in his personal relationship with Jesus Christ, who has forgiven him permanently. Corey can continue serving his patients, full of joy and purpose. He is free from harboring any prolonged grief or animosity because he practices forgiveness rooted in Christ. And so can you.

Forgiveness Not to Be Outwitted by Satan

Paul warns of another reason for practicing forgiveness. There is real danger involved in harboring grief or animosity on the front lines. As a CHP, we must practice forgiveness often, so we avoid becoming an easy target for being outwitted by Satan. Satan wants to stir chaos and discord in our relationships. He will do anything to tempt us to question our purpose, to consider quitting, or to consider the possibility that our love for Jesus has nothing to do with effective health care. He wants us to be hung up on the hurt we have experienced or that we have caused. He wants us to be slow to forgive and quick to harbor anger or hate. In other words, Satan wants to distract us from effectively representing the light of Christ where it is needed most.

Let's consider what would happen if Adi and Corey did not practice forgiveness. Suppose Adi became upset with herself for taking so long to figure out Frank's underlying issues. Suppose she gets upset with the psychiatrist and other doctors who treated Frank through the years. She realizes they prescribed Frank antipsychotic medications without treating him holistically. If anything, the medications may have masked the influence of his childhood trauma. If Adi does not forgive herself and her colleagues, her guilt will make her an easy target for Satan. Satan can then use her guilt to tempt her to question everything about her practice. She could become anxious in fear of making more mistakes and losing the joy she has maintained through the years.

Now suppose that Jeff Tanner, in the heat of his hurt and anger, went on a tirade, yelling profanities and mocking Corey. Only this time Jeff's words really got under Corey's skin. For some reason the mocking just struck a nerve and Corey stewed over Jeff's words the rest of his day, replaying them in his head over and over. If Corey does not practice forgiveness, the hurtful words will take root, and he will become an easy target for Satan. Satan can use the harbored grief or animosity to tempt Corey to question his purpose, to question his competence, and to doubt his role as a servant of common grace.

How long do you think Adi and Corey would last functioning under such dark thoughts? We have worked with enough colleagues in similar situations to predict that they will not last long. And, in the meantime, if they stay and do not practice forgiveness, there will be other consequences. They will be tempted to self-medicate (we see this way too often), to detach their practice from their beliefs, to stop caring for patients and colleagues, or to change jobs looking for a geographic cure. Instead of looking for opportunities to comfort and forgive, the shroud of dark thoughts will have them looking to survive each shift. Again, we have seen too much of that in practice.

Anchor your joy in Christ. Minimize the opportunity for Satan to wreak havoc on you, your patients, and your colleagues. Get comfortable practicing forgiveness so that you persevere and thrive for a long time as a CHP. Every day in humility, lay aside any resentment and allow God to use you to minister to others in practice. You will grow in your relationship with Jesus as you reinforce the dependence you have on his love and his forgiveness. You will also shape the culture of work at the hospital, clinic, or agency. Your joy and willingness to forgive will become contagious, creating a practice milieu conducive to the grace of God shining in even the darkest circumstances. Isn't that the kind of an environment where practicing health care is the most enjoyable and patients receive the best care?

A Practice Milieu of Joy and Forgiveness

The practice milieu can influence just about everything in health care. For example, a family clinic operating in a frantic, unfriendly environment would be a miserable place to work. There will be high turnover and patient care will suffer. Take that same clinic, incorporate staff committed to serving full of joy and practicing forgiveness, and the practice milieu will improve. Paul writes in 2 Cor 2:14–15, "But thanks be to God, who always leads us in Christ's triumphal procession and through us spreads the aroma of the knowledge of him in every place. For to God we are the fragrance of Christ among those who are being saved and among those who are perishing."

We want your witness to be one in which you are part of the fragrance and aroma of Christ where patients and colleagues feel loved. To enhance your witness, try incorporating the following steps related to forgiveness.

Practice Personal and Professional Forgiveness

The integration of personal and professional lives matters for CHPs. It is counterintuitive for Christian men and women to leave their personal lives at home and their professional lives at work. God is Lord of all our lives. The psalmist writes, "The LORD will send his faithful love by day; his song will be with me in the night—a prayer to the God of my life" (Ps 42:8). Our effectiveness as servants of common grace grows out of a personal relationship with Jesus Christ lived out in fellowship with all the people in our lives. Our husbands, our wives, our children, our parents, our friends, as well as our patients and our colleagues are all part of those toward whom we live out the greatest commandment. Jesus tells us in Matt 22:37–40:

> He said to him, "Love the Lord your God with all your heart, with all your soul, and with all your mind. This is the greatest and most important command. The second is like it: Love your neighbor

> as yourself. All the Law and the Prophets depend on these two commands."

Being intentional about practicing personal and professional forgiveness is a primary way of loving God and loving your neighbor as yourself.

Recognize and be accountable for your influence on the practice milieu. Just as the joys from home can spill over into your work, so can the griefs and resentments. When you practice forgiveness, you let God use the brokenness at home or in your community to expand your capacity for love, mercy, and grace as a CHP. Practice forgiving those closest to you in your family, your church, or your friend group, so you are at full capacity for the patience and the love necessary to represent God on the front lines.

Forgive Repeatedly

Just how much or how often should you expect to forgive as a servant of common grace? Perhaps as often as you breathe. Thank goodness you can live knowing that your sins are permanently forgiven. You now live in eternal fellowship with Jesus Christ. But the fruit, the purpose of your relationship with him, is to now live in such a way that others may come to know him as the Messiah. As Paul writes, opportunities to practice forgiveness are a test of the measure of obedience in your relationship with the Lord (2 Cor 2:9). Jesus makes it clear that there are no limits on forgiveness. Here is his interaction with Peter in Matt 18:21–22:

> Then Peter approached him and asked, "Lord, how many times must I forgive my brother or sister who sins against me? As many as seven times?" "I tell you, not as many as seven," Jesus replied, "but seventy times seven."[2]

---

[2] Some contemporary translations such as the ESV and NIV read "seventy-seven times" due to a connection to Gen 2:24, with the point being the same, endless forgiveness.

But why does Jesus require us to forgive so often? For our context, why do you as a CHP have to forgive so often? Why is it part of your spiritual competency to forgive so often? The answer is that the more you forgive others (and yourself), the more you will remember what Christ did for you on the cross. The more you forgive others, you give evidence of your faith in Jesus Christ who puts no limits on forgiveness, keeps no record of wrongs, and loves unconditionally with a pure heart. Forgiving people are grace-filled people. Your mindset toward practicing forgiveness as a CHP needs to be as innumerable as your desire to be a source of joy is infinite.

Separate Forgiveness from Consequences

Forgiveness does not preclude us and others from experiencing the consequences of sin. As a pastor, I (Jason) have sat and talked with families or individuals about the full forgiveness of Christ as a place of hope, while they or a loved one are also experiencing the effects of sin. As a CHP, give yourself permission to practice forgiveness in every circumstance or situation, no matter how depraved, by separating the two. Remember, we must comply with the code of ethics of our respective professions. We take an oath to treat or serve anyone needing care, regardless of the circumstances. If you practice health care long enough, you will provide care to people who are genuine scoundrels and/or have done really bad things. You will treat the offenders and the abusers of domestic violence. You will treat the perpetrators and the victims of sexual crimes. You will treat people incarcerated for heinous violent crimes.

As a CHP, you are in a unique position. You serve on the front lines where you get to be a servant of common grace to everyone. Embrace the reality that you may be *THE* person God uses to make himself known to patients. Practice forgiveness no matter the circumstances. Leave the consequences to the Lord. In some instances, you may be part of the consequences patients experience from their sins, their griefs, their hurt, and their poor decisions. In other instances, your care of patients may help them cope with the consequences. There will be times when all you can do is care for patients as they experience consequences (e.g., pain management). At other times, the care you provide may help restore patients from consequences. Regardless of the circumstances, persevere and thrive with joy by keeping sight of why you are there and whom you serve.

Embrace Being His Conduit for Forgiveness and Comfort

What a life we get to live serving others in health care. The time and energy invested in developing the professional competences of our respective fields grants us unprecedented access to share the gospel through our words and actions. The ability God gives some men and women (believers and non-believers) to provide care is evidence of his presence, making it clear in all our consciences that we are his creation, and that he is intimately involved in the care of our lives. Indeed, he is sovereign, reigning over every single hair on our heads (Matt 10:29–31).

If you are fortunate enough to represent him as a CHP, always keep your relationship with Jesus Christ at the forefront of why he has you there. You are to be an example of his immense patience for those who would believe and receive eternal life, and grounds for his judgment for those who hear his voice and do not believe (1 Tim 1:16; Heb 3:7–19). Embrace being his conduit for comfort and forgiveness so you can be his most effective example. That is how you can best direct the attention of patients and colleagues beyond the temporary glory experienced in health care to a *greater glory* in Jesus Christ. We use the next chapter to focus on our role as servants of common grace to always point patients and colleagues toward a greater glory.

You Are Not Alone: Help from the Past

Augustine, the fifth-century North African pastor, had struggled with guilt during his early days because he had not embraced the Christian faith of his mother, Monica. He later wrote that he was aware that his sinful choices hurt others, including his faithful mother. However, he did not yet understand that at the heart of the Christian faith is forgiveness. Once Augustine converted to Christianity (that story is retold in the previous chapter), he recognized the fullness of God's grace and mercy. He also had a deep appreciation for how Christ and his sacrifice was central to a Christian's hope in forgiveness. In his book *On Christian Doctrine*, Augustine uses medical imagery to explain how Christ became human so that he could heal sick sinners. He writes:

> Moreover, as the use of remedies is the way to health, so this remedy took up sinners to heal and restore them. And just as surgeons, when they bind up wounds, do it not in a slovenly way, but carefully, that there may be a certain degree of neatness in the binding, in addition to its mere usefulness, so our medicine, Wisdom, was by His assumption of humanity adapted to our wounds, curing some of them by their opposites, some of them by their likes. And just as he who ministers to a bodily hurt in some cases applies contraries, as cold to hot, moist to dry, etc., and in other cases applies likes, as a round cloth to a round wound, or an oblong cloth to an oblong wound, and does not fit the same bandage to all limbs, but puts like to like; in the same way the Wisdom of God in healing man has applied himself to his cure, being himself healer and medicine both in one. Seeing, then, that man fell through pride, he restored him through humility. We were ensnared by the wisdom of the serpent: we are set free by the foolishness of God. Moreover, just as the former was called wisdom, but was in reality the folly of those who despised God, so the latter is called foolishness, but is true wisdom in those who overcome the devil. We used our immortality so badly as to incur the penalty of death: Christ used His mortality so well as to restore us to life.[3]

[3] Augustine, *On Christian Doctrine*, 1.14.13.

Augustine understood that true life includes the freedom of forgiveness. Any Christian forgiveness is based in the merit of Christ and the grace that God has shown in forgiving us in Christ. Forgiveness from Christ and forgiveness given to others on the account of Christ frees the believer to live, and to love and serve others.

You Are Not Alone: Help from Above

As you are coming to grips with the beauty of the forgiveness that is offered to us and how those who are forgiven turn and forgive others, pray this with us:

> *Lord, you are the God who forgives. Would you help me to be an advocate for forgiveness in my healthcare setting? I need forgiveness from you and to rejoice in the full pardon that you give me because of Christ. I need your help to release my claims for vengeance against those who have wronged me. Help me to be the means that you use to help my coworkers and patients know the freedom and healing that is found in forgiveness. I pray, Heavenly Father, that you would forgive my sins as I forgive those who have sinned against me. In the name of Jesus, in whom we have been forgiven. Amen.*

Reflection and Discussion Questions

1. Think of patients you have worked with in the past. Can you recall at least one patient situation where the consequences of bad personal decisions and/or actions contributed to their presenting issues? In a small group, take time to share about the situations.
2. Now can you think of at least one patient where the grievous thoughts, actions, or decisions of others influenced the situation? Again, take time to share the details of the situation with others in a small group.

3. We shared the profound statement that *health-care practice is caring for patients who have grieved others and have been grieved by others, and it is done by by CHPs who have grieved others and have been grieved by others.* Does that statement resonate with you? Does it challenge you? Do you disagree? Does it offend you? Why?
4. How would you describe the practice milieu where you work as a CHP? How close does it come to being a place full of joy and forgiveness? What can you do to improve the work culture so patients and colleagues can experience the fragrance and aroma of Christ's love? Can you make a commitment to do one small thing the next time you are at the clinic/hospital?
5. What hurt, pain, and/or resentment are you holding onto in your life? How do you think it influences your health-care practice? Is there someone you need to forgive? Do you need to forgive yourself for something you said or did? Would you stop what you are doing right now, get down on your knees, and pray to the Lord? Confess to Jesus the wrong, the hurt, the pain you feel and/or caused. Thank him for nailing it to the cross for you. Forgive.

Chapter 6

A Greater Glory

For if what was set aside was glorious, what endures will be even more glorious. —2 Cor 3:11

Melissa Barnett: A Flight Nurse

Melissa has wanted to be a nurse for as long as she can remember. Her desire to help people was evident over the course of her childhood, into her teenage years. Graduating from nursing school was an accomplishment but just the beginning of her journey. Melissa worked in a variety of health-care settings, mostly critical care. In the emergency department setting, she had become very familiar with confronting and dealing with emergencies, both minor and severe. In the intensive care setting, most patients were comatose and on the brink of death; mortality became an even greater reality. The care Melissa rendered in the ICU was difficult but more often directed toward family members. These years were formative in growing her daily walk with Christ.

After ten years of gaining a plethora of knowledge and experience, Melissa applied for a flight nurse position at a level 1 trauma center and was offered a position. Melissa was at the pinnacle of her career. Orientation as a flight nurse was grueling and one of the toughest eight weeks Melissa had ever endured (second to six weeks of basic military training). Daily prayer and dependence on God's strength was foundational in learning a myriad of intense protocols and "lifesaving" procedures, always rooted in safety of the flight crew and the patient. After eight long weeks, orientation was completed and Melissa was finally living her dream: she was officially a flight nurse!

While Melissa's professional role was growing, her spiritual journey was also rapidly flourishing. Every shift started with a conversation between her and Jesus. Not one shift ever unfolded the same, but every flight started with "dropping of tones" which indicated that a flight had been activated and Melissa had three minutes to get to the helipad and prepare for the flight. Immediately after "tones" dropped, Melissa made her way to the helipad, completed pre-flight safety checks, and secured herself in the jump seat. She was the primary nurse on this scene flight and started mentally preparing for whatever may unfold. A big part of her mental preparation included dialogue with Jesus—flight nursing had directly impacted an open line of communication with her Savior (a practice that stands strong today). Melissa prayed for safety for first responders, comfort for patients and their family members, bystanders and witnesses of the emergency incident, and wisdom for care providers.

As the helicopter circled the landing zone, Melissa scanned the area for any hazards. Much to her surprise, she saw about 200 yards of burnt and smoldering grass on the shoulder of the road that was scattered with debris. Near the end of the scorched path were the remains of what appeared to be a vehicle that had literally been split in half and resembled a huge, shredded aluminum can. Melissa's thoughts about this scene became more intense as this was definitely the worst emergency scene she had ever seen.

After safely landing, Melissa and her partner were directed to their patient, Zeke, an eighteen-month-old male who was securely strapped in a car seat. However, the car seat had been ejected during the motor vehicle crash and Zeke was reportedly unresponsive. A quick primary assessment revealed a young toddler perfectly secured in his car seat who was not breathing and had no pulse. Melissa and her partner immediately removed Zeke from his car seat and strapped him to the flight stretcher while providing CPR. Baby Zeke was quickly loaded and secured in the aircraft for transport to the children's trauma center, where he could get advanced lifesaving care.

Baby Zeke's situation became surreal, but Melissa methodically rendered lifesaving care; she placed a breathing tube without delay while her partner was rendering chest compressions. Next, she attempted to start an intravenous line, but baby Zeke's body was in shock, and finding peripheral IV access was not possible—no worries, she would obtain intraosseous access. Melissa tightly gripped the intraosseous needle and tried to insert the needle in his little tib/fib and the needle bent. Melissa grabbed a second needle and tried again; the needle would slip off the bone, would not break through the tough bone, and again bent from the intense force required during the insertion attempt. Melissa was beyond frustrated and found herself pleading with Jesus to allow success in these lifesaving attempts. Melissa and her partner switched roles; while Melissa was performing chest compressions and providing breaths to her patient, she was scanning his entire limp body. This is when she realized Baby Zeke's angelic appearance. His skin color was pale, he was perfect in every way, and did not have a single scratch, bruise, or outward explanation to explain why he was limp and without life. Melissa remembers begging the Lord to explain why this angelic toddler was in this predicament. She pleaded with God to help her understand.

Paul Scaglione: Hospice Social Worker

Paul changed careers in his mid-thirties. After twelve years in corporate banking, he realized he wanted to help people instead of staring at spreadsheets all day. Upon finishing his MSW degree, he accepted a social work position at a hospice agency. As a licensed social worker, he works with patients who receive a life expectancy prognosis of six months or less to live. Upon receiving a referral, Paul meets with patients within twenty-four hours to assess the full range of their biophysical, psychosocial, and spiritual needs. He then builds a holistic treatment plan to help them access a wide range of services and resources to improve their quality of life. In short, in lieu of curative treatment, his purpose is to give patients and their families the wraparound support they need to ensure the best quality of life in their remaining time together. He is also the person on the medical team who helps counsel patients and families as they cope with the difficult emotions, relationship issues, and logistics involved at the end of life.

He received a new referral on Thursday evening after normal business hours. The oncologist from Memorial Health made a referral for Harris Tolley, a forty-three-year-old male with stage 4 Hodgkin lymphoma. Based on the results from the last PET scan, the oncologist determined that Mr. Tolley's treatment would focus on palliative care from this point forward. Paul was at the hospital the following morning to meet Mr. Tolley and his family. The initial plan was for Paul to prearrange the initial resources needed for Harris to be discharged that afternoon. Paul arranged for a medical bed to go into the living room on the first floor of their home. He also set up a visit from a hospice volunteer on Saturday afternoon to give his wife time to go to the grocery store. Paul then planned to follow up on Monday to meet with Harris and his family to talk about additional resources needed to keep him comfortable. The meeting on Monday never happened as Harris died at home early Sunday morning in his living room.

Making Sense of Our Limits

Melissa Barnett and Paul Scaglione experienced a phenomenon that every CHP encounters. They experienced the limits of their ability to care for patients. If you spend any consistent time working in health care, you will experience this phenomenon as well. It actually happens more than most of us want to admit. Most of us work in health care to help people. Yet, regardless of our credentials, how much training we complete, how skilled we are, or how much education we have, we will work with patients seeking care and will be helpless to help. Patients will respond unexpectedly to medications or treatments. Patients will take their own lives. There will be complications in surgical procedures or in patients' response to anesthesia. Patients will get sick, their illnesses will progress rapidly, and we will realize there is nothing we can do for them. Then we will work with patients who experience traumatic events who may heal physically but seem to continue suffering emotionally. In all these moments, it can feel as if all the years of schooling, residence, clinical rotations, internships, and experience seem useless or meaningless. In a sense, all of it *CAN* really be meaningless. There is certainly evidence from Scripture where the Lord reveals that apart from him it is all meaningless (e.g., read Ecclesiastes 1–6). But the Lord also reveals another way of making sense of our limits in light of the gospel of Jesus Christ. The other way is to:

1. Recognize the relationship between fading glory and permanent glory which reorients our view of competence and adequacy; and
2. Point people to the sufficiency of God who alone made a way for a greater permanent glory.

Pointing patients and colleagues to his permanent glory is the third spiritual competency. But first let us take a deeper look at the relationship between fading glory and permanent glory.

Relationship between Fading Glory and Permanent Glory

Paul emphasizes the relationship between fading glory and permanent glory in the third chapter of 2 Corinthians. Read below and see how he contrasts the two:

> Are we beginning to commend ourselves again? Or do we need, like some, letters of recommendation to you or from you? You

> yourselves are our letter, written on our hearts, known and read by everyone. You show that you are Christ's letter, delivered by us, not written with ink but with the Spirit of the living God—not on tablets of stone but on tablets of human hearts.
>
> Such is the confidence we have through Christ before God. It is not that we are competent in ourselves to claim anything as coming from ourselves, but our adequacy is from God. He has made us competent to be ministers of a new covenant, not of the letter, but of the Spirit. For the letter kills, but the Spirit gives life.
>
> Now if the ministry that brought death, chiseled in letters on stones, came with glory, so that the Israelites were not able to gaze steadily at Moses's face because of its glory, which was set aside, how will the ministry of the Spirit not be more glorious? For if the ministry that brought condemnation had glory, the ministry that brings righteousness overflows with even more glory. In fact, what had been glorious is not glorious now by comparison because of the glory that surpasses it. For if what was set aside was glorious, what endures will be even more glorious. (2 Cor 3:1–11)

The verses focus on the key difference between the law (tablets/letters of stone) related to the Mosaic covenant (see Exodus 20) and the gospel (the new covenant) proclaimed by the prophets and apostles. The law was divinely instituted. It came with glory. However, like the face of Moses, the glory of the law was transitory. The laws could not save. The laws related to the Mosaic covenant, which the people failed to keep (see Exodus 32 and many other Old Testament texts). All those legal demands could do is lead to condemnation and the need for a greater, permanent glory. There was nothing wrong with the law. The law was for human good. Our sinful nature, however, relegated what was good to bring about our death, so that our sins might become "sinful beyond measure" (Rom 7:13). The gospel of grace found in the new covenant is the greater, permanent glory as it brings atonement, righteousness, and eternal salvation. The author of Hebrews says that "the law perfected nothing," but Christ offers a new "better hope" through the new covenant (Heb 7:19). Instead of laws written with ink on tablets, the Spirit of the living God is now written on the hearts of men and women who believe in Jesus Christ.

As NT scholar Paul Barnett explains, "Thus 'death,' arising from disobedience and its accompanying 'condemnation,' characterizes the old covenant, whereas 'life' accompanying 'righteousness' and 'the Spirit,' enabling and empowering obedience to God, characterizes the new covenant." Barnett continues that the Spirit is "the fulfillment of the prophetic promise and prime blessing of the new covenant."[1]

The permanent glory of the gospel of Jesus Christ surpasses the fading glory of the Mosaic law in every way. The law requires the works of men and women to meet the perfect and righteous standard of a holy God. Unrighteous people always fall short of the needed righteousness. Faith in Jesus Christ is the only way to meet the standard. A personal relationship with Jesus Christ through faith allows us to be declared righteous and to have eternal fellowship with the Lord. The demands of the law are important in revealing the holy nature of God and keeping human society from pursuing our selfish and destructive desires. But the works of the law have a temporary effect and do not commend us to God.

As is the case today, letters of recommendation and/or the thoughts of others were a common part of first-century society. Paul wants the people in the church of Corinth to be a "living letter" that recommends the gospel to their neighbors because their lives reflect God's grace and the life of faith. Paul writes to distinguish between the limited value of the constraints of the Mosaic commands and the Spirit-enabled life found in the new covenant. He wants the believers in Corinth to find their confidence and their competence in Christ. He does not want them putting their faith in themselves or their works as that kind of faith leads to death. The works of grace of the

---

[1] Paul Barnett, *The Second Epistle to the Corinthians*, NICOT (Grand Rapids: Eerdmans, 1997), 183–84.

new covenant produce greater glory. Stated differently for us as CHPs, only through faith in Jesus Christ can people receive permanent healing, permanent peace, and permanent well-being.

Recognizing the relationship between fading glory and permanent glory has direct application for CHPs. It is a matter of what we acknowledge and emphasize in our health-care practice. Where do we get our confidence? What makes us competent? Are we competent in ourselves or does our competence come from God? Professional competence comes from the extensive training, credentials, certifications, and practice experience in our respective fields. Both Christians and unbelievers can develop the ability to help patients through prescribing the right medications and treatment regimens. Both can perform the right surgical procedures and provide the necessary rehabilitation. Only CHPs rightly view their professional competences as fading glory. Only CHPs understand the healing and care provided as being temporary. Though these temporary qualities have value, they point to the need for more. Only CHPs have the indwelling of the Holy Spirit, which helps them discern the reality of a permanent greater glory through Jesus Christ.

The indwelling of the Holy Spirit changes everything about how CHPs view their health-care practice. Jesus explains to his disciples that those who believe in him will receive the Holy Spirit who teaches us all things, goes out from the Father, and testifies about the Son (John 14:15–26; 15:26). As a disciple of Christ, you have the Spirit of truth in you who makes it possible to understand your health-care practice in relation to fading glory and permanent glory. Every part of health care, even the creation and presence of health care, is a form of fading glory. Health care is a fading glory because it all relies on the work of humans and can only bring temporary (and often imperfect) results. The advances in medications, the advances in treatments, and the advances in technology used in health care cannot escape the general corruption of creation that occurred because of the fall. Therefore, the function and purpose of health care as a form of fading glory must be understood in its relationship to its role in God's revealed plan of salvation.

Health care, in some ways, is a foretaste of the glory of God but fades rather quickly. When we help patients recover from illness or heal from injuries, their renewed health is only temporary. When we help patients survive trauma, loss, and grief, their feelings of restoration will disappear. It is as if God provides CHPs constant reminders of our mortality and limitations of the flesh. When it comes to health care, we can never let our medical knowledge and skill, developed from years of preparation, become an idol or a high place that usurps God. So, as important as it is to treat patients with the most sound and effective practices, as servants of common grace, our confidence and competence must always come from God. Here is a gruesome image to help visualize the difference. The fruit produced from health care practiced only from the perspective of fading glory is "The Walking Dead" (like the television show). The fruit produced from health care practiced with clarity of competencies of "fading glory" and "permanent glory" is an invitation to eternal salvation.

Let's reexamine the cases of Melissa Barnett and Paul Scaglione assuming they understood the relationship between fading glory and permanent glory. Recall that it was clear that Melissa seemed to have a personal relationship with Jesus Christ. Her role as a flight nurse appeared to heighten her sense of dependence on the Lord, placing her confidence in God above her training. She was flourishing in both her professional role and her spiritual journey. Her work as a flight nurse meant her practice was with patients facing life-threatening or life-changing injuries. She was intentional about integrating her relationship with Christ with all her training, experience, and skill to save as many patients as possible.

The motor vehicle accident that killed Zeke was devastating. Melissa did all she could to save this little boy. She also pleaded with God to save him. When it was clear that Zeke was dead, she then begged God to help her understand. Amid the chaos, she seems aware of her role as a servant of common grace. She even prays for potential patients, family members, and bystanders as part of her preparation for each shift. It is as if she engages in an open dialogue with Christ as she steps into life-and-death situations.

Though she couldn't save Zeke, she provided the best temporary care possible, while remaining conscious of God who alone made a way for permanent glory.

Paul Scaglione's relationship with God is unclear. If we assume he knows Jesus as Lord, the purpose of his role as a hospice social worker is clear. He provides holistic, wraparound care for patients who know they are likely going to die within the next six months. The purpose of his care is twofold. He engages, assesses, and intervenes with patients to care for their temporary needs, while reinforcing, one last time, the insufficiency of the works of the law to save. Through his care, he also affirms the reality of Jesus as Savior for those who believe. Although not stated in the case, the rapid set of events with patients like Harris Tolley is more than a rare occurrence. As he does with all patients, Paul used his training and experience to develop a rapport with Mr. Tolley and his family quickly, complete an assessment of the situation, and implement a plan to address needs. Although Paul never had the opportunity to follow up and engage further with everyone, his professional competence allowed Mr. Tolley to spend his last day alive in the comfort of his home surrounded by family. What an image. Perhaps the most people can expect living out their days in the here-not-yet relationship between the fading glory of this life and the permanent glory of eternal salvation through Jesus Christ our Lord. What a blessing it is for us as CHPs, serving as servants of common grace, to point people toward the latter in our interactions with patients on the front lines.

Pointing Patients and Colleagues toward Permanent Glory

Now we can focus on the third spiritual competency. When you experience the limits of helping patients, remember you are there for more than providing temporary care. You are there as a witness to the sufficiency of God who alone made a way for a greater permanent glory. But how do you become an effective witness of the Lord? How do you become effective at pointing patients and colleagues to permanent glory? Well, this competency is not like a professional skill or a technique that you can develop. The only way you become an effective witness of the Lord is by the Holy Spirit transforming you into a disciple of Jesus Christ, which makes you an effective witness of the Lord. The Holy Spirit teaches us all things so that we remember all that we know about Jesus (John 14:26). The Spirit helps us in a moment of trial or pressure to have the right things to say as a witness of Christ (Matt 10:19–20). And one of the central things Jesus teaches us is that he is the vine, we are the branches; if we abide in him, we will bear much fruit. But apart from him we can do nothing (John 15:5). What you *can* do is align your heart and mind to abide in him by living in joyful obedience to his will for your life. Below are several ways you can align your heart and mind with the Lord in joyful obedience. Your commitment to spending time in God's Word is key as the other ways become possible as the fruit of the Holy Spirit.

Let His Word Inform Your Training and Your Practice

By now it is probably obvious that we believe it is essential for CHPs to spend time in God's Word every day. Through a relationship with Christ, God made a way for all who believe in his Son to have direct access to him through the Bible. Here is perhaps the main point of our book. If you see yourself as a CHP and want to be an effective servant of common grace, we want you to approach your time in God's Word as central to your life. We want you to let God's Word have preeminence over everything that goes in and out of your soul. Why? Because we are confident that, through his Word, God will give you the eyes to see and the ears to hear to bear much fruit for him on the front lines. We are confident that if you seek God through his Word regularly, you will thrive, as you can endure anything that happens at the clinic, the hospital, or the agency. His Word will become a huge deposit in your mind and heart that you can draw from throughout the day in whatever situation you face. It will form your mind so that you think God's thoughts in a situation and have his words as you formulate your response in a given moment. His Word will form your heart so that your hopes and desires are shaped by his wisdom. Your work with your patients and interactions with your coworkers will seek to fulfill his purposes, not your own desires.

What we are recommending here is something beyond spending time in his Word. We are encouraging you to develop the discipline of letting God's Word inform your training and your practice. Although not meant to be prescriptive, here is one way you can develop the spiritual discipline for letting God's Word inform your training and practice. The psalmist declares, "I will meditate on your precepts and think about your ways. I will delight in your statutes; I will not forget your word" (Ps 119:15–16). As you go about your day in school or in practice, meditate and fixate your eyes on God's Word to inform and interpret how your relationship with God informs your practice at work. Do so by engaging in a meditation habit whereby you continuously seek to discern how Scripture influences all you think about and do as a CHP.

Look at the figure below (Figure 6.1). Notice the visual of the contemplative cycle we want you to incorporate in your health-care practice. Begin your days by spending time with God in his Word. As you read, pray to ask God to help you understand how his Word should influence what you will encounter in your days. Meditate on a few verses from your reading as you engage with patients and colleagues at work. At the end of your shifts, perhaps after dinner and/or spending time with friends and family, end your days by again spending time in the Bible seeking to discern all you learned and/or encountered through his Word. Now stay with us. What do you think will happen as you string together days, weeks, months, and then years building the basis of your health-care practice (along with all the other areas of your life) through the lens of God's Word? The Lord will align your heart and mind to be as effective as possible to point patients and colleagues to permanent glory through your words and actions.

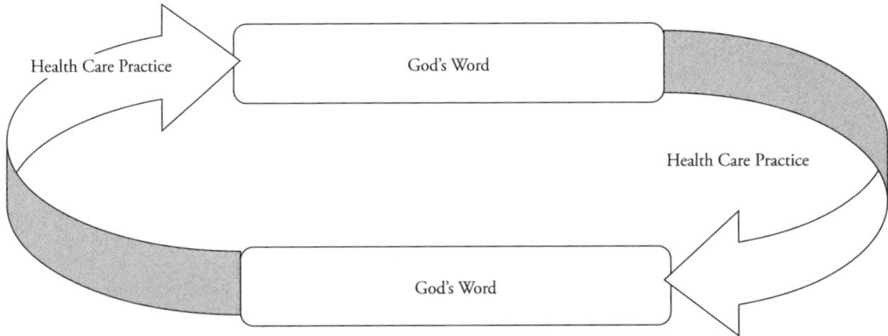

Figure 6.1 Contemplative Cycle to Inform Your Training and Your Practice

Consider Melissa Barnett as an example. She is certainly an experienced CHP. Let's assume that she delights in spending time in Scripture regularly. She has developed the discipline of beginning and ending her days by reading God's Word. Suppose the morning before meeting Baby Zeke, Melissa just happened to be studying in chapter one of 1 Peter. These were the words she focused on as she headed for work, and these were the words she read again at the end of her dreadful day:

> Blessed be the God and Father of our Lord Jesus Christ. Because of his great mercy he has given us new birth into a living hope through the resurrection of Jesus Christ from the dead and into an inheritance that is imperishable, undefiled, and unfading, kept in heaven for you. You are being guarded by God's power through faith for a salvation that is ready to be revealed in the last time. You rejoice in this, even though now for a short time, if necessary, you suffer grief in various trials so that the proven character of your faith—more valuable than gold which, though perishable, is refined by fire—may result in praise, glory, and honor at the revelation of Jesus Christ. (1 Pet 1:3–7)

How do you think God's Word might influence the way Melissa processes or discerns what happened to her on the front lines that day? What if

Paul Scaglione also began and ended his days reading Scripture. Suppose he just happened to be studying Psalm 103 the day he met Harris Tolley and his family. Do you think God's Word might reinforce his hope and faith in the Lord? How?

Display Boldness in Hope

Your active faith displayed in joyful obedience will shape how you are seen at work. Jesus makes it clear that we are to let our lights shine so others may see our good works and give glory to God (Matt 5:16). Begin viewing yourself as a beacon of hope when you arrive on the front lines. Be intentional to allow your love and trust in the Lord to seep into all you are doing. Know that when you go to work, you have a right to be full of hope because of what you get to do with your life. Regardless of the circumstances, you get to step into the lives of people to care for them. You get to provide care knowing that whatever confidence you have as a CHP to treat patients, you have even more confidence in God who provides a way to eternal salvation.

That kind of rugged, unflappable hope will be on display for everyone you encounter on your shifts. With that kind of hope, the roller coaster of ups and downs you experience in health care can't break you. Sure, like Melissa and Paul you will have difficult days. But as you remain steadfast in your faith, steadfast in your time with God in his Word, and steadfast in your purpose, more and more patients and colleagues will see your boldness in hope and joy on display. Some may even wonder and ask how you can be this way. Just be ready to point them to the source of your hope and do it with gentleness and respect (1 Pet 3:15).

Unveiled Freedom

Your faith in Jesus Christ, the source of your hope and joy, also allows you to practice health care with an unmeasurable degree of freedom. Christ frees you from seeking to make a name for yourself. He frees you from allowing your education, your credentials, your income, and your practice to become an idol that defines you. You focus on your relationship with Christ lived out in serving patients and colleagues and God will sort out and provide all the things you need to be his servant of common grace. Notice we are not suggesting that all the things that allow you to practice health care are unimportant. What we are suggesting is that you are free from the bondage of being enslaved to those things. Paul writes in Gal 5:1, 13–15:

> For freedom, Christ set us free. Stand firm, then, and don't submit again to a yoke of slavery.
>
> For you were called to be free, brothers and sisters; only don't use this freedom as an opportunity for the flesh, but serve one another through love. For the whole law is fulfilled in one statement: Love your neighbor as yourself. But if you bite and devour one another, watch out, or you will be consumed by one another.

As a CHP, when you work with patients and colleagues, let them see how unencumbered you are to love them and serve them as you would yourself. The life you live in the flesh you live by faith in Christ who loved you and died on the cross for you (Gal 2:20).

He freed you from succumbing to the fate of too many of our colleagues who have lost their way. Apart from Christ, it becomes too easy to get burned out from all the politics in health care. It becomes too easy to turn to self-medication or other destructive methods to escape from stress. It becomes too easy to allow ambition to zap their joy in serving others. In contrast, when you're practicing with unveiled freedom, placing your confidence in Christ, making him preeminent over your professional practice, you will most certainly point others toward permanent glory. Why? Because everything you're doing to serve the temporal needs of patients will serve as evidence of being cared for by someone transformed (and being transformed) as God's adopted son or daughter.

Transformed into His Image

Here is where faith in Christ shifts the approach to health care for followers of God. While CHPs use our professional training and competencies to care for patients, the trials and challenges on the front lines serve as a means for transforming us into his image. The more we are transformed into his image, the more effective we become at pointing patients and colleagues to permanent glory. The false dichotomy between the professional and personal fades away for the CHP. There is no need to waste time or energy trying to maintain the arbitrary separation between the two. There is only the Holy Spirit bringing about integration of all of our lives, transforming us into disciples of Jesus Christ.

What do disciples of Jesus look like? Here are a few characteristics from Scripture. Jesus called his disciples to deny themselves, take up their crosses, and follow him. His disciples become more and more willing to lose their lives for his sake knowing they will find it in him (Matt 16:24–25). His disciples do nothing out of selfish ambition or conceit. They actually count others more significant than themselves. His disciples take no confidence in their flesh. Instead, they consider everything as rubbish because of the surpassing worth of knowing Christ Jesus as Lord (Phil 2:3; 3:7–8). His disciples serve in joyful obedience, knowing they are being transformed by the renewal of their minds to discern the will of God and be made into the same image as Jesus Christ (Rom 12:2; 2 Cor 3:18).

Are you one of his disciples? Do you see evidence of the Holy Spirit at work in you? When you reflect on your life thus far, can you see his faithfulness through various blessings, trials, and challenges? Do you see how he has taken (and is taking) the brokenness of your life in the flesh and transformed it with his Spirit? He is making you into a jar of clay by which his light shines out of darkness pointing the way to his glory. The ironic truth of pointing to the permanent glory of the gospel is that since the true glory is God's alone, often the best means of displaying this permanent glory is through humble clay jars. Understanding and embracing how God is making you into a jar of clay is where we pick up in the following chapter. This is the next spiritual competence necessary to serve as an effective servant of common grace.

You Are Not Alone: Help from the Past

Early Christians tried to strike the balance of valuing the physical health that medical practices offered, and the greater glory of spiritual health offered in the gospel. Basil was a fourth-century pastor in Cappadocia (modern Turkey) who was a leading voice in establishing the church's trinitarian orthodoxy and in establishing a monastic rule that was used throughout the eastern church. His "rules" not only influenced Christian monks in the east but also became guidance for Christian piety for all Christians. Basil said that physical healing provided a useful analogy for spiritual healing. Drawing on the medical practices of his day, Basil says that some sicknesses were treated by withholding certain habits or foods and others were treated by "indulging" in healthy practices or foods. Spiritual health comes from withdrawing from sinful practices and increasing spiritual nourishment. Basil writes:

> Certainly, as was said before, those who have contracted illness by living improperly should make use of the healing of their body as a type and exemplar, so to speak, for the cure of their soul; since abstention from that which is hurtful according to the rules of the medical art, the choosing of what is beneficial, the observance of prescriptions, are of advantage to us also [in the spiritual life].[2]

Basil also points out that in certain situations the practice of medicine made some radical improvements in a person's physical health. This progress was symbolic of the type of improvement that can come to someone's spiritual

---

[2] Saint Basil, "The Long Rules" in *The Fathers of the Church: A New Translation*, Volume 9, trans. M. Monica Wagner, *Saint Basil's Ascetical Works* (Washington D.C.: The Catholic University of America Press, 1962), 336.

health. He also said that the giving and receiving of medical help still acknowledges that the ultimate power of healing rests with God:

> Further, the very transformation of the body from sickness to health should be an incentive to us not to despair of the soul, as if it had not power to be restored again through penance from its sinful state to its proper integrity. So, then, we should neither repudiate this art altogether nor does it behoove us to repose all our confidence in it; but, just as in practicing the art of agriculture we pray to God for the fruits, and as we trust a ship's captain in the art of navigation, but pray to God that we may end our voyage unharmed by the perils of the sea, so also, when reason allows, we call in the doctor, but we do not leave off hoping in God. It seems to me, moreover, that the medical art is no small aid to continency. I observe that this art prohibits sensual indulgence, it is opposed to overeating, it forbids as inexpedient an elaborate diet and an exaggerated liking for condiments. In general, it regards restraint as the mother of health, so that even in this particular its counsel is not without value for us. Therefore, whether we follow the precepts of the medical art or decline to have recourse to them for any of the reasons mentioned above, we should hold to our objective of pleasing God and see to it that the soul's benefit is assured, fulfilling thus the Apostle's precept, "Whether you eat or drink or whatsoever else you do, do all to the glory of God."[3]

Basil's pastoral counsel in this selection concludes with the encouragement for us to see anything done as a potential to bring glory to God. Even mundane, everyday items like eating, drinking, bandaging a wound, caring for a hospice patient, and counseling a young mother are all things that can be done to the glory of God.

---

[3] Basil, *The Long Rules*, 337 (modernized). The scripture citation is 1 Cor 10:31.

You Are Not Alone: Help from Above

As you are considering engaging the daily habits of your health-care practice seeking God's greater glory, pray this prayer with us:

> *Lord, you will be glorified throughout the world. Would you help me to seek your glory over my own in my health-care setting? I need the wisdom to keep the temporary healing that health care can bring in perspective to the greater glory of you as the healer of mind, body, and soul. I pray, heavenly Father, that you would strengthen me against the temptation of making my health-care practice about me, focusing on glorifying my strengths, or being embittered by my weaknesses. In the name of Jesus our Sufficient Savior. Amen.*

Reflection and Discussion Questions

1. Can you recall at least one situation where a patient was seeking your help, and you were helpless to help? Can you think of at least one situation where a patient responded unexpectedly to medications or other treatments? In a small group, take time to share about the situation.
2. Do you ever think about work as being meaningless? Do you ever feel as if you are just going through the motions? What have you done in the past to cope with the limits and shortcomings you experience working in health care?
3. Meet with a brother or sister in Christ. Practice describing what you do in health in connection to the relationship between fading and permanent glory. What would you share?
4. Practice using the contemplative cycle. First read Psalm 103. Now reread the case of Paul Scaglione. Can you describe how God's Word might influence the way Paul Scaglione views his work with Harris Tolley and his family?

5. Meet with another believer or meet in a small group with other CHPs. In your own words, can you describe what it means to practice health care in joyful obedience? Can you describe how the indwelling of the Holy Spirit changes your health-care practice?

Chapter 7

Jars of Clay

Now we have this treasure in clay jars, so that this extraordinary power may be from God and not from us. —2 Cor 4:7

Lloyd DiSalvo: A Psychiatrist

Dr. DiSalvo is a CHP who serves as the medical director of a community mental health center in an urban setting. The population the mental health center serves is comprised of people from lower socioeconomic backgrounds which compounds their vulnerability. Not only is the population challenging, but recently two of Dr. DiSalvo's associates retired early. Those two well-respected physicians left medicine earlier than planned because of COVID and the adverse effects it placed on the entire healthcare system.

While Dr. DiSalvo thoroughly enjoys caring for patients, he has come to realize that the lack of access to care is worse than ever. Workday hours have been extended and meeting patients' needs has become what seems an impossible task. All areas of health care have been affected post-COVID, but mental health issues are rapidly increasing while trained mental health professionals are scarce.

This morning at the monthly medical staff meeting, Dr. DiSalvo's mind is spinning as the performance improvement committee presents a myriad of protocol violations. While he wants to shout, "How can we follow practice guidelines and provide high-quality, safe patient care, when we are stretched beyond limits?," given the current reality, he knows finding and hiring more staff is an unlikely possibility. He also recognizes that he is ultimately responsible and must lead in all circumstances. He wonders how much longer he can continue to practice and serve as medical director under these conditions. Though he wonders, he also feels compelled to continue serving. He cannot bring himself to abandon his patients and colleagues.

Breanna Cooksey: Athletic Trainer

Breanna never intended to go into health care. Her junior year of high school she was a heavily recruited point guard who could do it all. She had the size, the athleticism, the shooting, the ball-handling, the court-vision, and the internal competitiveness to play basketball at the highest level. Her life-course changed on a snowy Friday evening in January in a small rural gymnasium. In the second quarter of a close conference game, Breanna drove the lane heading for a layup. Three defenders collapsed around her as she sent a no-look pass to the opposite baseline where her teammate hit an open three-pointer. Right as she passed the ball, however, she stepped on the foot of one of the defenders, spiraled hard to the floor, and lay grimacing in pain as she held her left knee. The following morning in the hospital she learned that she had torn her ACL and MCL at the same time. After surgery, her rehabilitation took fourteen months. She missed the rest of her junior year and most of her senior year. When she returned to play in the last few games of her senior year, she was just not the same.

Breanna never went on to play basketball in college. During the course of her rehabilitation, she discovered a new plan for her future. All the time and energy spent recovering from her injury introduced her to athletic training as a health profession. Breanna became fascinated by the anatomy of the knee, the rest of the body, and physical and psychological factors that influence performance. Perhaps most importantly, she valued the relationship she developed with the athletic trainer at her school who invested so many hours helping her recover. After high school, Breanna enrolled in college to study sports medicine. Five years later, she graduated with her Master's of Athletic Training. She now practices health care as an athletic trainer at an orthopedic medical practice that contracts to provide athletic trainers to several professional sports teams and colleges in the area.

Jane Morgan: A Nurse

Jane works on the medical intensive care unit (MICU) at St. Luke's Hospital. She has been a nurse for eighteen years and has spent almost all of it working at the hospital in one capacity or another. She joined the MICU staff seven years ago when they had an opening on the second shift. She is now the lead nurse on the unit during that shift.

Jane needs to work a second shift to fit her schedule. It is the only way she can manage all she has going on in her personal life. At work she cares for patients who are critically ill and have need for constant monitoring. Her shift begins by meeting with the lead nurse from the dayshift to review all patient records. She then makes a plan to carry out doctors' orders for everyone on the unit. Toward the end of her shift, she reviews patient records with someone from third shift. Jane enjoys taking care of patients. She also enjoys the relative peace and calmness involved in working on the unit. Her personal life is anything but calm and routine.

Her upper-middle class suburban home looks like an oasis from the road. The pristine cut grass, the basketball hoop in the driveway, and the "welcome home" sign on the front porch may portray the typical family life awaiting her when she gets home. What all of it really symbolizes is Jane's sacrifice to provide for her five children. The two youngest have Down syndrome. They are both low-functioning and can barely do anything for themselves. At thirty-one years of age with five toddlers at home, Jane's husband was killed in a freak accident while he was out hunting. Jane's life turned upside down as she lost the love of her life and she now had to find a way to bring in an income and take care of her family. Now with teenagers at home, two with special needs, her personal life is overwhelming and exhausting from the time she gets off work until she begins her next shift.

Her mom watches the kids when she is at work. Jane usually gets home between 11:30 and midnight. If she is lucky, she will get five or six hours of sleep. It all depends on whether or not the two youngest kids sleep through the night. She gets up at 5:30 a.m., spends a few minutes reading the Bible, then gets the oldest kids off to school. She then makes breakfast for the two with Down syndrome, gets them settled into their routine, and then gets started on paying bills and handling all of the chores around the house. Around noon, she makes herself and the kids some lunch. If the weather is nice, she takes the kids to the park. If not, she will take them to the local YMCA to play. At 1:30 she goes home so she can get ready for work. She also tries to be there when the older kids get home from school so she can spend a few minutes finding out about their day. She is out the door at 3:00 to get to work on time. Jane can't remember the last time she had a day to herself, a relaxing vacation, or even time to watch a movie that didn't involve cartoons or animation. Her two youngest children will likely need her to care for them into adulthood.

Different Types of Brokenness, Same Source of Light

Here is a picture with words to illustrate CHPs serving as servants of common grace. Visualize an army of caretakers, reconciled by Jesus Christ, radiating the light of permanent glory, shining through their diverse vessels of brokenness. Dr. DiSalvo is feeling the demands mounting at the mental health center. Yet he continues to serve. The only reason Breanna is a CHP is because her athletic dreams were crushed to pieces. She now provides care for others hoping to live out their athletic pursuits. Jane cares for patients at the hospital while living under the pressure of providing for her family and having to raise her children on her own.

Take a closer look at the picture. Zoom in on some of your classmates, mentors, and colleagues. Tune in and think about the various trials, the difficult situations, and the circumstances they have endured. Think about the professional and personal suffering they continue to endure. All of them seem to have every reason to pack it in and leave the front lines for good. But something keeps them going back. Moreover, the very things that would make most people stop, over time seem to make them even more effective, more resilient. It is as if they are given access to an infinite source of light that has them continuing to serve, even thrive, in joyful obedience.

What about you? Are you in the picture? If you're a student, will you be someone the Holy Spirit prunes and transforms from the depths of your brokenness into a vessel that shines light on the front lines? If you recently accepted Jesus Christ as Lord and Savior and you're already working in health care, will you be in the picture? Do you want to be in the picture? Now that you are reconciled to God for all of eternity, how will your unique trials and challenges shape how you reflect his light? Will you continue serving in joyful obedience? Your faithfulness to continue serving Christ in joyful obedience as he transforms you into one of his jars of clay is the next spiritual competency.

Commit to showing up ready to practice health care every day, regardless of what happens, and God will make you a conduit of his light amid darkness.

His Light amid Darkness

Let's consider what is happening when CHPs care for patients. On one hand, the care offered by CHPs to patients is like any other health-care provider. The willingness, the knowledge, and the practical ability necessary to attend to the temporal needs of patients is, on its own, a common grace. On the other hand, something unique is taking place when CHPs treat patients. As much as CHPs bring their training and expertise to patient care, they have been entrusted with something much more important—so important that it takes priority over anything else we can do for patients. Why? Because it is the only way (the only treatment) for anyone to receive eternal salvation/permanent healing/the most effective health care. Paul makes this point in his second letter to the church of Corinth. He states:

> For we are not proclaiming ourselves but Jesus Christ as Lord, and ourselves as your servants for Jesus's sake. For God who said, "Let light shine out of darkness," has shone in our hearts to give the light of the knowledge of God's glory in the face of Jesus Christ. (2 Cor 4:5–6)

Paul has no interest in communicating any personal value about himself or his abilities to the church of Corinth. His perspective is that since meeting Jesus on the road to Damascus (see Acts 9), he is now a servant of the Lord. Just as Jesus emptied himself in joyful obedience to his Father's will to save his people, Paul empties himself so that he can always point others to Jesus. He considers his religious heritage, his training, his professional status as meaningless apart from the light of God. The light of God has been imbedded in his heart by the Spirit and points others to permanent glory (2 Cor 3:17–18). For all believers, the Spirit utilizes our weaknesses and intercedes for us while at the same time helping us to be conformed to the pattern of Christ's life (Rom 8:26–30). It is by the Spirit that believers are transformed from the image of the old human nature into the image of Christ ("the man of heaven" in 1 Cor 15:49).

The verses are equally as relevant for you as a CHP. If you believe in Jesus as Lord and Savior, he emptied himself for you. You now have the indwelling Holy Spirit transforming you more and more into his disciple. Your transformation involves an emptying of self-importance for Jesus's sake. As a CHP, embrace that it is his light that shines in your heart that points others to his glory. Like Paul, begin to look at your personal life, your training, your credentials, and your professional status as meaningless apart from his light. In joyful obedience, make your love for Christ first in your life, even first in your health-care practice. Give God your hurts, your brokenness, your past trauma, your failures. God will shape you into the vessel that most effectively lights the way for patients and colleagues to know that healing and salvation through the blood of Christ is real.

His Healing Vessel

God uses the brokenness of frail lives to share the gospel of Jesus Christ. By choosing the weakest people and transforming them from the worst depths of brokenness into something useful, God points to his true, lasting glory. Paul viewed himself as the worst of all sinners whose suffering for the gospel was the Lord's intended means for sharing the truth about Jesus. He literally describes himself as a jar of clay that God is using to show others his eternal glory. For Paul, he expects to face suffering as he proclaims Christ. But he does not see his suffering as destruction or an end. Rather, he sees his suffering as a means of transformation and renewal for himself and for others hearing the gospel. As you read the verses below, contemplate the ways you see God transforming you like he did Paul into his healing vessel. Paul writes the following in 2 Cor 4:7–18:

> Now we have this treasure in clay jars, so that this extraordinary power may be from God and not from us. We are afflicted in every way but not crushed; we are perplexed but not in despair; we are persecuted but not abandoned; we are struck down but not destroyed. We always carry the death of Jesus in our body, so that the life of Jesus may also be displayed in our body. For we who live are always being given over to death for Jesus's sake, so that Jesus's life may also be displayed in our mortal flesh. So then, death is at work in us, but life in you. And since we have the same spirit of faith in keeping with what is written, I believed, therefore I spoke, we also believe, and therefore speak. For we know that the one who raised the Lord Jesus will also raise us with Jesus and present us with you. Indeed, everything is for your benefit

> so that, as grace extends through more and more people, it may cause thanksgiving to increase to the glory of God.
>
> Therefore we do not give up. Even though our outer person is being destroyed, our inner person is being renewed day by day. For our momentary light affliction is producing for us an absolutely incomparable eternal weight of glory. So we do not focus on what is seen, but on what is unseen. For what is seen is temporary, but what is unseen is eternal.

Paul's description should resonate with us as CHPs. Let's take a closer look at how God refines us to be his servants of common grace on the front lines in health care.

Treasure in Jars of Clay

God makes our refinement possible. He does something to us that is simply amazing. If you know in your heart and profess with your mouth that Jesus Christ is your Lord and Savior, God puts his permanent light (the Spirit) within you, making you alive. This treasure should change your perspective on health-care practice. Beyond whatever professional knowledge, value, and skills used to help patients, beyond any medications, surgical procedures, or treatments available to provide care, you are a conduit of his light to everyone you encounter. And, as a conduit of his Spirit (light), you bring with you to every shift, every setting, every exam, every patient/family consult, and every medical staff meeting, the all-surpassing power to save lives, to transform lives, and to bring complete healing and restoration.

The power you bring, however, is not your power. It belongs entirely to God. It is his permanent treasure that he puts in your finite body. As Paul puts it, "this is from the Lord who is the Spirit" (2 Cor 3:18).

Embracing the contrast between your physical competence and the work of the

Spirit through you is important. Why? So you can maintain a humble and eternal perspective of your purpose in health care.

The treasure is the gospel of Jesus Christ who conquered death. The vessel, the conduit of his light, is a jar of clay. *God is the treasure. You are the vessel.* You are an important but mortal container subject to the certainty of illness, decay, and death. In this way you are just like your patients and colleagues. One finite decaying, dying person helping care for the temporary ailments of other finite decaying, dying people. But God made you alive in Jesus, transforming your purpose in health care (Eph 2:4). Now you are God's healing vessel caring for the temporary ailments of other people as a living testimony of the permanent resurrection of life for those who believe in Christ. But always remember, you are just his healing vessel. God intentionally chooses to use you, a weak, lowly, and frail decaying conduit of his light, and he receives all the glory for his saving work. Your health-care practice is never focused on you, the jar of clay. It is always about him, the treasure, refining you as a testimony of his existence and power.

Hard Pressed, Not Crushed

As a perfect, infinite treasure concealed within broken finite vessels is how God refines those who believe in his Son. His treasure is always the source of health, redemption, and eternal life. We, in our flesh, are not. His treasure is perfect. It never needs to change. It never needs to adapt. Rather, his treasure causes us, his vessels, to adapt to become more like his perfect treasure. In 2 Cor 3:18 it is pictured as the glory of Christ now becoming more of what we look like and will eventually be complete ("from glory to glory"). In 2 Corinthians 4 Paul uses different metaphors to describe the divine paradox that occurs when we become more like his perfect treasure. The divine paradox is that Paul's suffering for the sake of the gospel of Jesus

Christ brought healing and renewal for himself and those he reached in ministry. The metaphors are equally relevant for describing how God refines us as CHPs.

Paul begins by stating that we are hard pressed on every side, but not crushed. He knew just how difficult and dangerous it was to proclaim the gospel. He experienced almost unimaginable hardships such as hunger, beatings, imprisonment, poverty, sleeplessness, and sorrow (2 Cor 6:4–10). Toward the end of his life, he even knew that he would eventually die for what he believed (2 Tim 4:6). In joyful obedience, he continued putting himself on the front lines to share the good news of Jesus Christ in words and actions. Feeling burdened to reach as many people as possible, he endured to the end. As a CHP, you can too.

Take note, you *will* feel hard pressed on every side at some point working in health care. Though you may never experience some of the same hardships as Paul, you are serving the Lord in difficult and troubling circumstances. The factors that create the context for health-care practice make it inevitable. Serving on the front lines with people who are hurting, being a constant reminder of mortality, and having to uphold ethical codes of conduct that necessitate serving all patients predisposes you to being hard pressed on every side. Add in the people and experiences from other parts of your life, and you should come to expect hardships.

Perplexed, Not in Despair

You *will* become perplexed, but not driven to despair. There is a legitimate reason why some of your colleagues, even ones who would say they believe in Jesus Christ, are tempted to separate their spiritual beliefs from their practice. There is enough to worry about between the complexities of the human body, the medications and treatments, and the politics and finances involved in the health-care system. Why complicate practice further by incorporating their beliefs? There is always the safe fallback (or cop-out) available where they rationalize that one's spiritual beliefs are personal. They can try to convince themselves that the hospital, the clinic, the agency, are not appropriate places for health-care professionals to integrate their beliefs. The allure of keeping patient care as transactional and impersonal as possible is real. It seems more clinical and may be thought of as compliance with corporate policy. We might have landed on a position of personal choice. If patients believe in God and it helps in their care, great. If not, that is fine as well. It's totally up to patients to decide for themselves.

There is a problem with trying to approach practice this way. You just cannot leave things alone. Your relationship with Christ and/or your desire to understand how he fits into your practice was enough to keep you reading this far into the book. God *does* have you serving as a CHP for a reason. His Word *does* provide specific guidance on how your faith transforms your practice.

As a servant of common grace at the front lines, you are a conduit of his mercy.

As a jar of clay, you are a vessel for his saving grace, the gospel that shines into darkness. Jesus tells you in Matt 5:14–16 what he wants you to do with his light. He states:

> You are the light of the world. A city situated on a hill cannot be hidden. No one lights a lamp and puts it under a basket, but rather on a lampstand, and it gives light for all who are in the house. In the same way, let your light shine before others, so that they may see your good works and give glory to your Father in heaven.

The truth of Christ is the light. You can bear witness to that truth and be the light for a particular hospital or clinic. Like Dr. DiSalvo, your mind may spin as you endure the discombobulated mess of the health-care system. Help patients and colleagues see beyond and navigate through the perplexities. Rely on him as he will not let you despair.

Persecuted, Not Forsaken; Struck Down, Not Destroyed

The hardships in health care can become personal. You can do everything right. You can serve patients and colleagues through your respective health profession in good faith and with integrity. Some will still mistreat you. Some may file grievances against you. Some may sue you. In some instances, though you are doing good work, some may get rid of you. Paul expected people to persecute him and try to strike him down as he proclaimed Christ as the Messiah. The Lord even told Ananias, at Paul's conversion, that he would show Paul how much he would suffer for his name (Acts 9:15–16). If you are someone who believes that Jesus Christ is Lord and Savior, you should expect to be on the receiving end of persecution as well. As a CHP you are bringing your relationship with the Son of Man to the front lines. He wants you to consider it a blessing when people hate you, exclude you, and reject you because of him (Luke 6:22). Like Paul, take courage knowing that Christ will never leave you or abandon you (Heb 13:5).

We (Michael and Angie) have both experienced persecution as CHPs. The Lord was always faithful with us as we endured. For example, while working at a large community mental health center, I (Michael) treated patients with severe mental health and substance disorders in an outpatient partial hospital program. The program consisted of individual medication maintenance with several different group therapy sessions each day. Patients entered the program through referral after being discharged from an inpatient psychiatric unit or were admitted as part of a plan to prevent hospitalization. A significant number of patients entered the program as part of an effort to satisfy a local judge who sentenced them to complete treatment. One patient diagnosed with Bipolar I Disorder and Borderline Personality Disorder cursed at me repeatedly throughout her treatment. She completed the program, avoided hospitalization, and was able to function much better at the end. But for whatever reason, I was the target of all her animosity. Though it was difficult, I took refuge in the Lord (through time in his Word and prayer) knowing that I was helping patients exactly where he wanted me serving.

For twenty years, I (Angie) felt the Lord had me serving exactly where he wanted me as well. Things ended quickly. Though I had done nothing wrong, I experienced being struck down, but not destroyed. From 2010 to 2016, I saw patients as a nurse practitioner in a primary care clinic. I loved everything about my work and the partners who owned the practice. Things started to change during my last year there. Shifts in policies and procedures at the clinic took a turn toward cutting costs. Although the changes made at first had minimal impact on day-to-day operations, eventually they became more significant. I thought that patient-centered care was becoming compromised. Given my long tenure at the network and my relationship with the partners, I thought it was important for me to talk with them.

I never had the chance. Little did I know, business decisions were being made that did not include putting patient care first. One evening after getting home from work, without any advanced notice, I received a letter indicating that the practice had eliminated my position. I was devastated. I had never been terminated before. Going in the next day to get my things was about the most difficult thing I ever experienced as a CHP. At the time, I felt humiliated. Although it was difficult and perhaps unfair, I know that the Lord was with me through the whole ordeal. A different family medicine clinic hired me soon thereafter. Looking back at the situation, I know for certain that the Lord worked things out where my transition to the new clinic enabled me to continue providing the best patient care possible.

Given what we know about working in health care, there is a significant possibility that you *will* experience being persecuted or struck down professionally at some point in your career. Sometimes these hardships are explicitly because of your faith in Christ. We (Michael and Angie) both know from personal experience and from interacting with enough CHPs to know it happens too often. When it happens, we encourage you to avoid asking God "Why me?" Instead, focus on remaining in him through spending time in his Word and in prayer. He will not forsake you or let you be destroyed. Take Jesus's word at face value when he promises that as you remain in him, he remains in you. As he allows you to be pruned (or refined), you will bear much fruit in your health-care practice (John 15:1–4) for his glory and not your own.

Carrying the Death and Life of Jesus

The divine paradox now reaches the climax for what happens as we continue serving in health care as CHPs. As jars of clay (fleshly conduits of God's infinite light) that continue suffering on the front lines, we become evidence of the crucified Jesus to our patients and colleagues. Paul interprets all the hardships he endured in ministry as a kind of reenactment of the crucifixion. He describes in 2 Cor 4:10a that he was always carrying around in his body the death of Jesus. Paul knew that as he proclaimed Jesus there would always be those who rejected the message and those who became so offended that they would seek vengeance against him. Jesus promised that his disciples would be treated with the same contempt as he received (Matt 10:24–25). The same principle is relevant for us as CHPs. As we are intentional about integrating our relationship with Jesus Christ with our health-care practice, we should expect to experience suffering, and even hatred, because there are those who hate Jesus and all those who represent him. And, just like Paul, as we continue caring for people amid hardships, our willingness to persevere in joyful obedience becomes evidence of our faith in Christ and the source of our power to endure.

There is still another side of the paradox. Paul writes that he endures in carrying the death of Jesus in his body so that the life of Jesus may also be manifested. He further explains that followers of Christ are always being given over to death for a purpose—so that the life of Jesus may be on display in our own flesh (2 Cor 4:10–12). Just as the death of Christ led to the resurrection, our embodiment of his death leads to the manifestation of a resurrected life.

Again, there is direct relevance for us as CHPs. When the indwelling of the Holy Spirit allows you to develop the inner strength to persevere, even thrive, amid outer hardships, your life becomes evidence of your faith in Jesus. It is as if the infinite light of permanent glory is pulsing throughout your mortal body.

Your presence in health care is, therefore, essential and important regardless of your specific field or specialty.

There is now nothing about your practice that you should consider mundane or tedious. No matter how difficult or stressful things get, there is a reason to endure and keep going back to the front lines. The life of Jesus is shining forth through you, amid your weakness, as you persevere.

Your presence in the hospital, agency, or clinic means the life of Jesus is on display for everyone to see.

You are there serving faithfully in joyful obedience as one of his servants of common grace, treating the temporal needs of patients from the eternal perspective of the truth—Jesus is the only way to permanent healing and salvation.

Eternal Perspective for Temporal Affliction

Paul concludes his description of believers as jars of clay by offering the most wonderful assurance (reread 2 Cor 4:16–18). He does so by inviting followers of Christ to look at life from God's perspective. For believers in Jesus, as our finite selves waste away, God is renewing our inner selves day-by-day. Any hardships and suffering endured is just temporary and part of how God is preparing us for eternal glory. As Australian scholar Colin Kruse notes on these verses, "In the light of the prospect of a future resurrection and the grace that is presently extending to more and more people through his ministry (vv. 14–15), Paul does not give up. And he is further enabled to do so because he knows that, while his 'outer person is being destroyed,' his 'inner person is being renewed day by day' as he keeps his eyes fixed on that 'eternal weight of glory' being prepared for him."[1]

We are to live our lives by faith, not by sight. We want you to take God's assurance to heart as a CHP. Your faith is what will make you as effective as possible as a servant of common grace. Moreover, while your professional training allows you to attend to the temporal needs of patients, your testimony of faith in Jesus Christ as Lord and Savior is what makes permanent healing possible for everyone you encounter.

There is no reason to ever lose heart. You are his healing vessel. Whatever difficult circumstances you experience working in health care, be assured that the days and years of trials are nothing compared to the eternal joy that awaits you. Make it your priority to share your joy for the things that are unseen and eternal with patients and colleagues. In words and actions, be intentional to always point them toward your hope in grace alone, through faith alone, in Jesus alone. God bestowed an awesome privilege on you as a CHP. He sends you to the front lines amid the chaos as his ambassador for Christ. God is literally making his appeal to others by sending you to represent his Son. Embracing your identity as his ambassador is the final spiritual competency and the focus of the next chapter.

You Are Not Alone: Help from the Past

John Calvin, a preacher and theologian in Geneva in the sixteenth century, wrote biblical commentaries on most of the books of the Bible. In his comments on 2 Cor 4:7, Calvin noted that ministers of the gospel were not chosen because of any noble or preeminent quality. Instead, the humble status of ministers caused the glory of the gospel to shine as a treasure in an earthen vessel. Calvin explains:

> It is ordered by the special Providence of God, that there should be in ministers no appearance of excellence, lest anything of distinction

---

[1] Colin Kruse, *Exegetical Guide to the Greek New Testament: 2 Corinthians* (Nashville: B&H Academic, 2020), 97.

> should throw the *power of God* into the shade. As, therefore, the abasement of ministers, and the outward contempt of their persons give occasion for glory accruing to God, that man acts a wicked part, who measures the dignity of the gospel by the person of the minister.
>
> Paul, however, does not speak merely of the universal condition of mankind, but of his own condition in particular. It is true, indeed, that all mortal men are *earthen vessels.* Hence, let the most eminent of them all be selected, and let him be one that is adorned to admiration with all ornaments of birth, intellect, and fortune, still, if he be a minister of the gospel, he will be a mean and merely *earthen* depository of an inestimable *treasure.* Paul, however, has in view himself, and others like himself, his associates, who were held in contempt, because they had nothing of show.[2]

Calvin's instruction provides encouragement to all who want to be a witness for the gospel regardless of their rank, background, or past. As Calvin notes, God in his providence chooses weakness to display his strength and humble things to reflect his glory. As a CHP, you may serve people in physical brokenness and yet offer them something of eternal value. We may be fully aware of our weaknesses and fears, but the power of God enables his gospel to come to others through us.

You Are Not Alone: Help from Above

As you are considering how the Lord may use you as a witness for his life-giving gospel message, pray this prayer with us:

> *Lord, you will be glorified through the spread of your gospel throughout the world. Would you help me to be your faithful witness in my words and work? I need your protection from sinful distractions and evil pressures. Grant me protection from those who want to stop my witness for*

[2] John Calvin, *Commentary on 2 Corinthians*, trans. John Pringle in *Calvin's Commentaries* (500th Anniversary Edition) volume 20 (Grand Rapids: Baker Book House, 2009), 174.

your name, and give me courage in the face of any rejection or persecution. I pray, heavenly Father, that you would deliver me from the evil one and the evil influences around me. Help me not to dim the light of Jesus. In the name of Jesus, our Victor. Amen.

Reflection and Discussion Questions

1. Talk with a trusted CHP mentor or friend. Can you share your own unique experiences where it was evident to you that the Holy Spirit was pruning and transforming you from the depths of your brokenness into a vessel that shines his light on the front lines?
2. As you think of colleagues you work with (or students you're in class with), what do you know about their life story where the Holy Spirit was actively working in their lives, transforming them from a broken place into a vessel where his light shines on others? If you don't know enough about your colleagues (or fellow students), take the time to learn more about some of them in a genuine relationship. You may find out that you are working (or in school) with other jars of clay.
3. Can you describe things at work that you find perplexing? Things that just seem to make your job more difficult or you just don't understand? How are you able to continue? What keeps you going back to work each day? Why stay in school? What is helping you persevere?
4. Have you ever been the target of persecution? Have you ever been excluded, rejected, perhaps passed over for a position or a promotion? What do you think about this idea from Luke 6:22 that you should consider it a blessing when people hate you, exclude you, or reject you because of Christ? If you have had time to heal from the initial hurt, how has the experience changed or informed how you think about your work as a CHP now? Do you feel more emboldened and empowered? Any new biblical insights?
5. What would it look like for you to begin bringing an eternal perspective to your work as a CHP? How might that perspective influence your interactions with patients?

Chapter 8

Ambassadorship

Therefore, we are ambassadors for Christ, since God is making his appeal through us. We plead on Christ's behalf, "Be reconciled to God." —2 Cor 5:20

Sydney Woodburn: Physician Assistant

Sydney loved two things as a teenager. She loved learning about God, and she loved anything to do with health care. The youngest of five, her parents pulled her out of public school after the fifth grade. She was homeschooled with her brothers and sisters until she graduated. Throughout her education, her parents encouraged Sydney to find ways to invest in her passions. Sydney went on multiple mission trips where she volunteered in orphanages and medical centers in different countries. She also attended medical camps in the summers on the campus of two different Christian universities. When it was time to go to college, she attended a Christian university in the Midwest that emphasized biblical integration. She completed an undergraduate degree in allied health. Two years later she graduated from the same school with her Physician Assistant master's degree. For the last six years, she has worked in family medicine at a rural health clinic affiliated with a large regional hospital network. She also continues serving at a hospital in Zimbabwe each summer as part of a medical missions team sent by her local church.

Sydney keeps a fairly regular schedule working at the rural health clinic. She is there 7:30–4:30 Monday, Wednesday, Thursday, and Friday. She gets to work a few hours later each Tuesday as the clinic stays open until 7:00 in the evening. Working in family medicine requires Sydney to be ready to work with many different patients. She cares for male and female patients of all ages over the course of their lifespan, diagnosing and treating illnesses and injuries related to every organ system. There are no typical days for her. She can perform annual checkups, manage patients with chronic conditions, and even perform minor surgical procedures all in the same day. Today, her last appointment in the afternoon is with Blake Simmons, who is at the clinic for his annual sports physical.

Blake Simmons is a rising senior in high school. At six feet five inches tall and weighing two hundred and sixty-three pounds, he is a starting defensive end for his high school football team. Blake has already earned just about every honor and accolade the past three years on the team. This year he is in striking distance of becoming the all-time sack leader for the state. He is also being heavily recruited to play football in college. However, before he can step on the field, he needs to have his annual sports physical just like every other student-athlete. Sydney completes his medical history and physical examination. She asks about medical problems in the family, any previous hospitalizations or surgeries, and any allergies, past injuries, and current medications. She also asks Blake specific questions about his history with smoking, vaping, alcohol use, drug use, or performance enhancing supplements, including steroids. She then completes his physical examination. After determining that Blake is a healthy young man cleared for playing, she concludes her exam by signing his form.

Dan Evans: Nurse Anesthetist

Dan is an experienced nurse anesthetist. For the last eighteen years he has worked at a Level I regional hospital. He typically works first shift from 7:00–4:00 five days a week. Once every two weeks he is on call, which requires him to be within thirty minutes of the hospital in the event he is called in for an emergency surgical procedure where another anesthetist is needed. Dan arrives at work most days around 6:00 in the morning, giving him plenty of time to change into his scrubs and learn about where he is assigned. He then meets with his assigned interdisciplinary surgical team, reviews the patient records, and preps all the medications he will potentially need throughout the day. Dan begins the current shift assigned to neurosurgery where he will care for Mr. Burkett, who is scheduled for cervical discectomy and fusion surgery.

Mr. Burkett is a seventy-two-year-old man bothered for years by progressive pain and stiffness in his neck and back. After exhausting all nonsurgical treatments, he and his doctors decided cervical fusion was necessary as he recently began experiencing burning pain and numbness spreading down into both of his legs. He arrived at the hospital early that morning. At 7:00 a.m. he was waiting in his bed in pre-op when Dan walked in to see him. Dan introduced himself to Mr. Burkett and his wife. He then explained his role as the one who would administer the anesthesia, monitor his anesthesia during the operation, and be there to manage his recovery from the medications after the surgery. Dan administered 2 mg of midazolam. A few minutes later, he was in the operating room ready to administer and monitor the general anesthesia.

The surgery took longer than expected. Although the surgeon told Mrs. Burkett that the procedure should take between four to six hours, complications caused Mr. Burkett to be in surgery for over ten hours. It took longer than anticipated to remove the disc between the c2c3 vertebrae and there was excessive bleeding during the bone extraction taken from his pelvis. Dan was there with Mr. Burkett all day maintaining the right dosing levels of anesthesia throughout the operation. When the surgeon finished, Mr. Burnett was moved to his room. Dan then began the emergence process, gradually discontinuing the medications so Mr. Burkett would regain consciousness. For the next hour Dan monitored him for any signs of agitation, persistent pain, or any respiratory problems requiring immediate treatment. Toward the end of his shift, Dan completed his necessary documentation, reviewed the case with the anesthetist replacing him for second shift, and introduced him to Mr. Burkett. He then said goodbye to Mr. Burkett and his wife, assuring them that he would most likely check in on them the following morning before the surgeon discharged them from the hospital.

Putting It All Together

We are now at a point in the book where we need to review what we have covered. Ambassadorship is the final spiritual competency, but it is much more. It is the culmination of what we are as CHPs. It is also the culmination of what we *do* as CHPs. Stated another way, ambassadorship becomes synonymous with our purpose for serving patients and colleagues needing our help. Ambassadorship is also the meta-competency that CHPs bring into play when God works in us to be faithful and effective with the other spiritual competencies. When we understand what is so unique about working in health care, why God has us there, and what guidance he provides from his authoritative and perfect Word, it transforms everything about our practice because our practice serves as evidence of our ambassadorship. Let's consider Sydney Woodburn and Dan Evans as we review.

Uniqueness of Working in Health Care

Remember the three factors that make health care a unique way to serve the Lord in ministry. First, *all CHPs serve patients on the front lines*. The work environments are stressful, the skills and the expertise needed are high, and the patients (people) seeking help are vulnerable. Moreover, all the people, the politics, and the costs involved in the health-care system can make it challenging to care well for patients.

Second, *all CHPs remind patients of their mortality.* Patients come to see us to prevent, treat, and/or cope with illness. The efforts of CHPs can bring temporary healing as our knowledge and skills of the body and mind help men and women cope with the fallout of our sin. However, from pediatrics to geriatrics we remind patients that eventually the breath of life will leave our flesh and we will return to the ground as dust.

Third, *all CHPs take oaths to follow specific professional codes of ethics.* CHPs always care for patients under the guise of following specific standards of ethical practice. As part of those standards, all CHPs take an oath to serve every person in need of help. Race, ethnicity, religious beliefs, nationalities, social class, sexual orientation, homelife, or any other variable has no bearing. Every patient can expect to receive competent, ethical care.

Sydney Woodburn serves people on the front lines. As a physician assistant in a rural health clinic, she is likely one of only a few trained medical professionals available to help people in that community. Although we do not know for certain, it is reasonable to assume that by the time she gets to Blake Simmons, she has seen patients all day needing various levels of care and treatment.

Sydney's examination of Blake seemed to be routine. She determined that he was a healthy young man cleared for football. But think about all that was involved in the physical examination. Think about all the information she gathered about him and his family. Sydney gets to know more about Blake than just about anyone else in his life. She also is responsible for making a comprehensive and sober assessment/decision that will determine if he is allowed to play. Think about how much is at stake for his life. Think about the consequences of Sydney missing something in the exam, for example an irregular heartbeat, and Blake gets overheated in practice and dies. Her exam of Blake, though routine, is still a reminder of his mortality. Lastly, Sydney must provide care regardless of his background, her like or dislike of football, or anything else she knows about Blake.

Dan Evans also serves on the front lines. Patients are completely vulnerable under his care. When patients such as Mr. Burnett need surgery, they are dependent on Dan for their very lives. Even as he tries to relieve their pain, he certainly reminds them of their mortality. He too has no say in the patients he serves. His role is to provide the same level of care to whoever is scheduled with him for surgery that day.

Why God Has Us There

Remember, God strengthens Christians working in the health-care professions for a specific reason. All CHPs serve people for a purpose beyond immediate healing and relief. Our divine purpose is to serve God as his servants of common grace. As his servants of common grace, God can use us to confirm for patients and colleagues that he is the Creator and Sustainer of all things and that his revealed Word is true. Recall that our interactions with patients and colleagues fulfill three specific objectives of common grace:

1. We prevent patients from experiencing the complete consequences of their sin.
2. We enable patients to experience temporary goodness and peace.
3. We help keep patients alive and healthy for as long as possible to hear the gospel.

Sydney Woodburn is a servant of common grace. She prepared for her purpose by completing her education at a Christian university emphasizing biblical integration. Her work with patients at the rural clinic and at the hospital in Zimbabwe each summer seem to represent the fulfillment of her faithful and joyful obedience to God since her adolescence. Dan's relationship with the Lord from the case vignette is unknown. Let's assume, however, that Dan recently confessed his sin and professed his faith in Jesus Christ as his Lord and Savior. Does anything change for him at the hospital? Should the way he works with patients and colleagues as a nurse anesthetist change? The answer is that whether he was ready or not, Dan is a CHP just like Sydney. His faith in Jesus Christ transformed everything about him, including his health-care practice. It has to. As Paul writes, "If anyone is in Christ, he is a new creation" (2 Cor 5:17a). Dan is a new person with a new purpose because he now has the Holy Spirit in him giving him new life. He and Sydney can read and understand God's authoritative and perfect Word. They both have access to the guidance they need to serve the Lord effectively on the front lines as servants of common grace.

Guidance from God's Word

God does not send us to the front lines empty-handed. He does not send us to the hospital, the clinic, or the agency serving as his servants of common grace, while leaving us alone to figure out what we are supposed to do. Our relationship with Jesus Christ gives us direct access to him in prayer. We have the Holy Spirit in us influencing everything about our lives, including our interactions with patients and colleagues. We are called by the same Spirit into "one body" with other believers (our local church) who will encourage us, forgive us, teach us, and serve with us (Eph 4:16). We are not alone or empty-handed.

By God's grace, we have an open invitation to learn and grow in our relationship with him through spending time in his Word. The Bible is one complete narrative where God reveals who he is to us, who we are in relation to him, who we are in relation to other men and women, and who we are in relation to the rest of creation. Within the context of the big picture of God's Word, the Lord provides specific guidance for aligning our hearts, our minds, and our actions with his purposes to make us as effective as possible as CHPs. As we are used to the language of "professional competencies" in our respective health professions, the apostle Paul describes four "spiritual competencies" that all CHPs should seek to embody in their health-care practice.

CHPs practice comforting others in their afflictions. *We comfort* patients and colleagues as an outpouring of the comfort we receive from God who comforts us in our afflictions. CHPs practice forgiveness. *We forgive* out of an abundance of love for the Lord and for those we serve. After all, health-care practice is caring for patients who have grieved others and have been grieved by others, and it is done by CHPs who have grieved others and have been grieved by others. *We point to greater glory*. We recognize the temporal limits of our abilities to care for patients. The best way to care for the health and well-being of patients is to point them to the sufficiency of God who alone makes a way for a greater permanent glory. *We serve as jars of clay*. We have the permanent, all-surpassing power of God's light (the gospel) within us to save lives, to transform lives, and to bring complete healing and restoration. Our health-care practice is never about us, the jars of clay. It is always about God, the treasure, refining us as proof of his existence to patients and colleagues.

Sydney Woodburn and Dan Evans are health professionals. They both completed years of extensive education and passed difficult licensure exams that enabled them to enter their respective professions. Their training and expertise give them access to serve alongside other professionals caring for patients. From a worldly perspective, they are just like their colleagues. From a biblical perspective, they are so much more. They are CHPs. And as CHPs, their personal relationship with Jesus Christ makes them special, obedient to a higher calling. Their presence in health care serves a more significant, eternal purpose. They are God's laborers sent out to his harvest on the front lines where people come face-to-face with their finite lives. Comforting others in their afflictions, practicing forgiveness, pointing toward a greater glory, and being his jar of clay are the spiritual competencies that will make them effective laborers. Why? Because as they practice those competencies, they attest to being servants of common grace and *his ambassador*, God's representative for his Son, Jesus Christ.

His Ambassador, His Representative

The apostle Paul was laser-focused on representing Jesus Christ as his ambassador. Since meeting Jesus, he no longer cared about how the world looked at him. He no longer sought their acceptance or approval. He cared about being faithful to sharing God's plan of reconciliation. His concern was for how people related to Christ. God reconciled humanity to himself by offering his Son as an atoning sacrifice in their place. Christ died taking on all our sin so that we can take on his righteousness. Anyone who believes in the resurrected Christ is freed from the bondage of sin and is now created new in Christ Jesus. Compelled by his love for Christ, Paul implored everyone on behalf of Christ to be reconciled with God. He writes:

> Therefore, since we know the fear of the Lord, we try to persuade people. What we are is plain to God, and I hope it is also plain to your consciences. We are not commending ourselves to you again, but giving you an opportunity to be proud of us, so that you may have a reply for those who take pride in outward appearance rather than in the heart. For if we are out of our mind, it is for God; if we are in our right mind, it is for you. For the love of Christ compels us, since we have reached this conclusion, that one died for all, and therefore all died. And he died for all so that those who live should no longer live for themselves, but for the one who died for them and was raised.
>
> From now on, then, we do not know anyone from a worldly perspective. Even if we have known Christ from a worldly perspective, yet now we no longer know him in this way. Therefore, if anyone is in Christ, he is a new creation; the old has passed away, and see, the new has come! Everything is from God, who has reconciled us to himself through Christ and has given us the ministry of reconciliation. That is, in Christ, God was reconciling the world to himself, not counting their trespasses against them, and he has committed the message of reconciliation to us.
>
> Therefore, we are ambassadors for Christ, since God is making his appeal through us. We plead on Christ's behalf, "Be reconciled to God." He made the one who did not know sin to be sin for us, so that in him we might become the righteousness of God. (2 Cor 5:11–21)

You are also Christ's ambassador. You step in as God's personal representative as you care for patients and colleagues. Pause for a minute . . . Now read the previous two sentences again. *You are also his ambassador. You step in as God's personal representative as you care for patients and colleagues.* Let the weight of those words sink into your heart and mind. Like Paul, we want you to be crystal clear about your motivations for serving patients at the front lines. Like Paul, we want you to trust that God's grace is sufficient to fulfill his purposes through you as his ambassador. Why? Being clear on your motivations and dependent on his grace will make you an effective ambassador.

God sends *you* to represent Jesus Christ, at the hospital, the clinic, or the agency. At a point when people are most vulnerable, you are serving and caring for patients representing the sacrificial love of Christ; God is making his appeal through you that all who put their faith in his Son are made new. The authentic love of Jesus Christ transformed your life and is transforming your life. You now can see beyond the outward appearance of things, to the eternal spiritual dimension of things. As Paul writes, "We walk by faith, not by sight" (2 Cor 5:7). Your best work as a CHP is but a foretaste, an example, or a demonstration of God's plan to reconcile humanity to himself, freeing us from enslavement to the world and to sin, and re-creating us in Christ. Paul says in 2 Cor 5:5 that the Spirit is given to us as a "down payment," meaning that the life change that has already happened is just a foretaste of the greater blessing of resurrected life. God's plan is to rescue all who believe in him from our human frailty, the same frailty that CHPs confront every day. Paul says that we all long for God to complete his work "so that mortality may be swallowed up by life" (2 Cor 5:4). What we really want as CHPs is for patients and colleagues to experience the gospel of grace that can give them resurrected life.

One Grace

Here we come full circle as Christians who take Scripture seriously and our health-care practice seriously. There is only one God. There is only one source of grace. God is a God of grace. You were once separated from God. Consistent with his character, God made a way to reconcile you to himself. He sent Jesus Christ, his only begotten Son, who died for all, that when you repented and believed in him, you were forgiven for your sins and made new in the image of Christ. You now live having received the assurance of eternal salvation and newness in life. Two parallel phrases in 2 Cor 5:18 picture our new status and new purpose: God "has reconciled us to himself through Christ and has given us the ministry of reconciliation." As NT scholar Ralph Martin comments, "The first part refers to the redeemer's work; the second half applies the benefits to the redeemed people."[1] In other words, having received Christ in your heart, you are a new creation of God with a new purpose. You are to be a servant or steward of his grace. You can't just keep it to yourself. You are to be his ambassador taking the message of salvation in Christ into every place you go.

You are a CHP. You represent God on the front lines in health care. You are to take the message of salvation in Christ into the hospital, the clinic, or the agency. Be clear on your purpose. Be intentional in your practice. Delight in God's Word. Let his Word influence everything about your practice. As Paul writes, "We make it our aim to be pleasing to him" (2 Cor 5:9). Pray for your patients.

Engage, assess, and treat patients as servants of common grace.

Be deliberate in comforting them in their afflictions, practice forgiveness, point them to permanent glory, and be his jar of clay relying on the sufficiency of God's grace to make you into his healing vessel. Paul provides the reasoning: "Therefore, since we know the fear of the Lord, we try to persuade people" (2 Cor 5:11). In everything you do in your health-care

---

[1] Ralph Martin, *2 Corinthians*, WBC, 2nd ed. (Grand Rapids: Zondervan, 2014), 298.

practice, do it imploring and hoping everyone you encounter is reconciled to God.

The Two Outcomes of Ambassadorship

Your role as an ambassador for Christ transcends your practice as a CHP. You focus on developing the unique expertise and skills needed to treat patients from within your respective profession. It is important that you have the training, the credentials, and the credibility that allow you to work in health-care settings. Your presence is needed so you can bring the good news. Beyond the core competencies of your profession, being an ambassador means bringing the good news of the gospel of Jesus Christ to the front lines. It is a blessing, a privilege, and a responsibility to be his ambassador. After all, the message you carry is of eternal significance and importance. Rely on the sufficiency of God's grace and he will make you effective as his representative. He will also fulfill his purposes through your joyful obedience and service.

His purposes are twofold. God will use your faithful service to reach some patients and some colleagues. He will also use your faithful service to leave everyone without an excuse. You love, serve, and care for every patient and every colleague in such a way to encounter Jesus Christ, and some will come to know him as their Lord and Savior. For others, though you cared for them, though you helped them, though you healed them temporarily, though you helped them cope and come out on the other side of hardships, though you shared your peace with God, they will never believe in Jesus Christ as Lord and Savior. All will stand before the Lord ready to give an account to him who is ready to judge the living and the dead (1 Pet 4:5–6). As Paul warns, "For we must all appear before the judgment seat of Christ, so that each may be repaid for what he has done in the body, whether good or evil" (2 Cor 5:10). When that final judgment comes, unbelievers will be unable to say they never had a chance to know him because when they needed care, they experienced you, the very representative of God.

Remember, God is responsible for the outcomes. There is no need to feel any pressure to discern which of the two outcomes God is accomplishing. You are his means of fulfilling both purposes. As a CHP, you are free to just love God and love others as you engage in professional health care. Just be prepared to always give the reason or source of your joy to anyone who may ask, doing so full of grace and seasoned with salt.

Love God So You Can Love Others

Loving God and loving others are what really matters as a CHP. The emphasis just seems so simple and obvious. You want to serve God effectively as his ambassador? You want to be a competent and effective Christian serving as a nurse, physician assistant, athletic trainer, physical therapist, pharmacist, dentist, social worker, or psychologist? You must love God and love others. Yes, that's it. But just how do you love God and love others? Well, begin by understanding that they are intricately linked. *You must love God so you can love others.* You must get the order right. It won't work any other way. God's Word tells us that it is the only way. Read this passage from Deuteronomy:

> Listen, Israel: The LORD our God, the LORD is one. Love the LORD your God with all your heart, with all your soul, and with all your strength. These words that I am giving you today are to be in your heart. Repeat them to your children. Talk about them when you sit in your house and when you walk along the road, when you lie down and when you get up. Bind them as a sign on your hand and let them be a symbol on your forehead. Write them on the doorposts of your house and on your city gates. (Deut 6:4–9)

Moses writes this passage in a time of transition. A new generation of Israelites were about to enter the Promised Land. Most of them did not really understand or fully grasp what their parents had to endure because of their lack of faith (Numbers 13–14). It was God's desire that things go well for them. They needed to be reminded of who God is, who they were in relation to him, and what he had done for them. Moses reviewed all that happened and all that God had done for them in the first four chapters of Deuteronomy. He then restates the law in chapter 5. In chapter 6, he begins addressing how they were to live, doing so by emphasizing the most important thing. He writes the Shema: "Hear, O Israel: The LORD our God, the LORD is one."

The Shema became the Jewish statement of faith. Jewish people are supposed to recite the Shema every morning and every evening. Also, for believers in Christ, this confession is a clear declaration of truth that there is only one God, that he created all things, and he alone is worthy of reverent fear. Reverent fear produces joyful obedience, love, and worship. It is a fear that comes about by considering who God is and all that he has done, and wondering like David:

> When I observe your heavens, the work of your fingers, the moon and the stars, which you set in place, what is a human being that you remember him, a son of man that you look after him? (Ps 8:3–4)

It is out of this faith and knowledge of who God is—producing reverent fear—that God wanted the Israelites to love him with all their heart, soul, and might. The narrative of the Old Testament reveals just how fickle the Israelites were in living out the greatest commandment. Sin made it impossible for them to get it right. Sin continues to make it impossible for us to get it right as well. True to his character and love, the Lord made the impossible possible through the life, death, burial, resurrection, and ascension of his Son, Jesus Christ.

Having faith in Jesus Christ as Lord and Savior is how you keep the greatest commandment of all. If you have faith in him, your old self was crucified with Christ, and you have been set free from sin. You are now to consider yourself dead to sin and alive to God in Christ Jesus (Rom 6:5–11). So when Jesus answers the scribes in Mark 12:29–31 with the Shema and then adds, "Love your neighbor as yourself," you now have the Holy Spirit within you to transform you into someone capable of keeping the greatest commandment, even on the front lines in health care. The apostle John helps believers see these connections in 1 John 4. He tells us that we can love God because he first loved us and "sent his one and only Son into the world so that we might live through him." John then adds that "if God loved us in this way, we also must love one another" (1 John 4:9–11).

You focus on loving God so you can love your patients and colleagues. But how does God want you to love him? The Bible indicates at least three things you can do to love God:

1. *Don't put any other gods before him.* The Lord is a jealous God (Deut 5:7–9). Don't allow any part of creation or any part of your life to become too important because it blocks out the cross. The Lord our God is the one and only God. Don't make idols out of positions, possessions, or people.
2. *Put God first.* Eventually, Christ will reign over everything and everyone. He calls us to surrender to him as Lord over everything in our life and over every part of our life (Col 1:15–20). For our purposes, Christ wants to be Lord over every aspect of your health-care practice. Avoid fitting God into your life and practice. Make God the priority and align your life and practice to him.
3. *Listen to him.* During the transfiguration (Matt 17:1–13), as Peter, James, and John were on the mountain, a bright cloud overshadowed them and a voice from the cloud said this about Jesus: "This is my beloved Son, with whom I am well-pleased. Listen to him!" (v. 5). Discerning how to listen to him happens by spending time studying his Word and spending time with him in prayer. The apostle John speaks about the confidence that we gain from God's Word. He explains, "I have written these things to you who believe in the name of the Son of God so that you may know that you have eternal life" (1 John 5:13). He continues by saying believers now have a confidence before God that "If we ask anything according

to his will, he hears us" (v. 14). When you love him this way, you align your heart, mind, and soul to him for the awesome blessing and responsibility of being an ambassador of Christ wherever you're serving as a CHP.

You Are Not Alone: Help from the Past

Charles Haddon Spurgeon, a nineteenth-century pastor in London, preached for decades in the heart of London and was a well-known preacher of the gospel. One part of Spurgeon's personal background compelled him to be a regular preacher of the gospel. As a young man, Spurgeon was spiritually searching and looking for answers. As he was headed to his regular church, bad weather diverted him to a Primitive Methodist church. Spurgeon entered the small church that snowy morning. The regular preacher could not attend due to the storm, so a lay preacher (a shoemaker or a tailor) shared a simple gospel message. Spurgeon was converted and would be forever committed to sharing that hope with others through decades of ministry. It is estimated in his decades of preaching that Spurgeon shared his conversion story over 200 times. Remembering the despair of being dead in sin makes a person's gospel witness relatable and compelling. Spurgeon writes:

> Why did God send ambassadors to men? He might have made peace without doing so, but he has chosen to put honor upon instrumentality and he has dealt with us as with reasonable beings. Further, why did God send men as his ambassadors? Would not angels have been better messengers? The probability is that an angel would have been quite unfit for such work as this. When a man, a sinful man who has himself been forgiven, talks to other sinners, he talks very tenderly and sympathetically;—at least, he ought to do so;—and when he meets with any distressed souls, he recollects the time when he was in distress; and when he hears about their doubts and fears, he remembers his own; and when he mourns over their rebellions,

> he recollects what a rebel he used to be; and therefore he is gentle with them, and longs that, if possible, peace may be made between the rebel and his God. But if an angel had been Christ's ambassador, after he had preached most earnestly, you would always be able to make this excuse to him, "Ah, you cannot enter into our feelings, for you have never had our temptations and trials."[2]

Spurgeon's comments about the relatability of one human who has been reconciled to God to another human in need of such a reconciliation will make sense to CHPs. In medical practice, a CHP is both a giver and a recipient of medical care. One of the reasons that CHPs can empathize with their patients is that at some point the CHP was the one in need of care.

Concluding Thoughts

We believe serving the Lord in a health-care profession is a unique way to spend your life. Patients and families come to you during periods of their lives when they are exposed to the sober realities of their brokenness and their mortality. Like other colleagues, you are there to care for their temporal needs. But you are also there as an ambassador for Christ. As his ambassador, the Lord makes his appeal through you, giving them the opportunity for permanent healing through Jesus Christ.

Maybe you have never viewed your health-care practice this way. Maybe you find yourself overwhelmed, burned out, or thinking of leaving the front lines for good. Maybe you have read this far, and you really want to embrace how God wants to use you at work. Maybe you just don't know where to begin. Let us encourage you to start by knowing that God has loved you and now calls you to love him.

---

[2] Charles Spurgeon, "Christ's Ambassadors" in vol. 11 of *Spurgeon's Expository Encyclopedia* (Grand Rapids: Baker Book House, 1988), 38. This sermon is based on the text of 2 Cor 5:20.

Begin by examining your life. Take note of people and things that you are treating like gods, that are becoming idols. Here are a few questions to help you discern this:

- What in your life is taking up too much of your time, attention, and/or energy that is keeping you from spending time with God in his Word?
- In what part (or parts) of your life are you not letting Christ be first?
- Is he Lord of your personal relationships?
- Is he Lord of your goals and ambitions?
- Is he Lord of everything you do in your health-care practice?
- If you are not a believer and for some reason you decided to read this far into the book, what is standing in the way?
- What false gods are you holding onto that are keeping you from confessing and asking Jesus Christ to save you right now?

You Are Not Alone: Help from Above

Pray with us:

> *Lord, thank you for the privilege and blessing to represent you in our practice. Lord, we thank you for who you are and what you have done for us. We thank you for the magnificence of everything you created. Lord, thank you for giving us your perfect Word. Thank you for giving us access to you through our faith in Jesus Christ. Jesus, we want you to be Lord over all our lives. We turn from the things in our lives that we are keeping from you, not letting you be first. Give us the courage to loosen our grip and let you have sovereign rule of every part of our lives. Help us to love you before everything else. Lord, pour your grace into us so that we may love those whom we encounter in life and our practice.*

If you have not yet trusted Christ as Savior, then we (Michael, Jason, Angie) pray this prayer for you:

Lord, we pray for anyone who reads this book, yet does not know you. God, initiate and lift the veil from their eyes so they can see Jesus for who he really is—your beloved Son who died on the cross to save sinners like us so we may be with you forever in permanent glory. Lord, draw them by your Spirit so that they may believe that Jesus is raised from the dead and that they will confess Jesus as Lord. We pray all this with confidence in the name of Jesus Christ, our Lord and Savior. Amen.

Reflection and Discussion Questions

1. Meet with a brother or sister in Christ or meet in a small group with other CHPs. In your own words, can you describe why God has you on the front lines in health care serving as a nurse, doctor, social worker, etc.?
2. When you go to work, you are there as a servant of common grace. You are also there as an ambassador of Christ. There is no inconsistency or contradiction in why you are there on the front lines. Can you articulate how both roles are connected?
3. In your own words, can you describe the two outcomes of ambassadorship? How does knowing the two outcomes help you serve patients and colleagues well?
4. Can you describe an interaction with a patient or colleague where, in your assessment of the interaction, you could have been more effective as a servant of common grace and an ambassador of Christ?
5. Take a moment and read Mark 12:28–31 on your own. Can you articulate how the verses could and should influence your approach to practice? Try to be as specific as possible. Now, revisit your response to the fourth question. Can you put in words what you would do differently in your interactions with the patient or colleague?

Chapter 9

Strategies for Thriving and Enduring

Finally, brothers and sisters, rejoice. Become mature, be encouraged, be of the same mind, be at peace, and the God of love and peace will be with you. . . . The grace of the Lord Jesus Christ, and the love of God, and the fellowship of the Holy Spirit be with you all. —2 Cor 13:11, 13

This is a book written by Christian health professionals (with the help of a theologian) for Christian health professionals. We sought to address two big questions for those who take Scripture seriously and their health-care profession seriously:

1. Is it important for Christians to serve in health care?
2. If so, does God's Word provide tangible guidance for what we are supposed to do as Christian health-care professionals?

We hopc and expect that if you have read this far, you know the answer is a resounding *yes* to both questions.

Addressing both questions is important. It is important because answering those questions serves as the basis for a comprehensive approach to biblical integration in our respective professions. Based on our own experiences and our own personal relationships with the Lord, we believe a comprehensive approach to biblical integration is important for thriving and enduring through the years of serving God in the harvest field of health care. The harvest is indeed plentiful on the front lines, but as you know, the laborers are too few. We want you to experience the blessing of serving God in joyful obedience in health care regardless of the circumstances. If you serve faithfully long enough in health care, you will likely witness the power of the gospel of Jesus Christ in tangible ways that many Christians may never experience. But you will also experience, both firsthand and vicariously, a variety of trials and suffering that many Christians may never experience.

We use this final chapter to highlight strategies for you to run your race well as a servant of common grace. The tips are really for any Christian wanting to grow in their relationship with God. We urge you as a CHP, however, to consider these as essential for avoiding burnout and being faithful servants on the front lines. We do not want you to think that this strength and wisdom comes from *something* within you but rather from *someone* within you. We begin by making sure you recognize the central importance and role of the Holy Spirit.

The Holy Spirit

The Holy Spirit makes it possible for you to thrive and serve God in joyful obedience in health care. It is the Holy Spirit who gives his power to the proclamation of the gospel. When you placed your faith in Jesus Christ as Lord and Savior, the Spirit led you to the confession of Jesus as God (Eph 1:17–19; 1 John 4:2). Based on the faith that unites us to Christ, God granted you eternal salvation, forgave you of all your sins, and gave you new life in the gift of the Holy Spirit (Rom 8:8–11; John 7:37–39; 8:23–24). The indwelling of the Holy Spirit inspires you to understand and believe God's Word (John 14:26; 16:12–15). His Spirit confirms in your heart that God loves you, that he considers you a fellow heir with Christ, and that you will receive what God has promised (Rom 8:14–17, 22–25; Eph 1:13–14). His Spirit is also how God empowers you to fulfill his purposes for you as a CHP and a part of the body of Christ (1 Cor 12:3–13).

Your purpose is to represent God as his servant of common grace on the front lines in health care. As a health-care professional, you must continuously seek to develop competence in your profession. However, as a servant of common grace, you do not necessarily "work" on thriving and enduring. Rather it is the Holy Spirit who works in you to prune, refine, and empower you with all that you need to become more effective in carrying out your ministry in health care. Lastly, it is the Holy Spirit who both moves you to incorporate the habits of grace (spiritual disciplines) and, at the same time, enables you to benefit from those habits. Keep a humble perspective. Incorporate the strategies below out of an authentic desire to love and grow in your relationship with Jesus Christ. Trust and have faith that the Lord will empower you through the Holy Spirit to fulfill your calling. Always be prepared to give him the glory and tell others about what he is doing through you, doing so with gentleness and respect. If you do, you will be effective, even when you don't necessarily feel as if you are effective. Your testimony will be clear because you will be keeping your relationship with the Lord first in all you do with patients and colleagues.

Strategy #1: Continuous Learning and Growing

Approach your professional discipline and your purpose in health care in a similar way—with a spirit of humility. You will never be completely trained and competent. You are always *becoming*. You are always becoming a competent nurse, a competent athletic trainer, a competent physician, a competent social worker, a competent pharmacist. In the same way, you are always becoming a competent and effective servant of common grace. As a CHP, you must seek to learn and grow in your respective profession and in your knowledge and relationship with God. Growing in both areas will keep you primed and ready to persevere. Make a commitment to further your expertise beyond what you already know. Never stop learning and growing. The new information learned will keep things fresh and give you the chance for new beginnings. Additional training may also allow you to expand into other areas to help more patients.

In the same way, seek to learn more about your relationship with God. We want you to saturate your life with the gospel of Jesus Christ. The gospel is not just one topic or one part of your life as a Christian and/or as a health professional. The gospel of Jesus Christ IS your life. Everything you learn and do happens within the gospel. The Bible is where you go to learn and grow in the gospel. Commit to spending time with God in his Word every day. Become a member of a local church body where you have access to solid preaching and teaching of the Bible. By solid preaching and teaching, we mean a church where the pastor(s) treats the Bible as the authoritative, sufficient, inerrant, living Word of God. Individually and corporately, prayer and reading God's Word are the core components of the Christian meditative cycle (see chapter 3) needed to inform your professional training and practice as a CHP.

Strategy #2: Develop a Robust Prayer Life

As a CHP, you must develop a robust prayer life. There are (or there will be) so many demands on your time and energy in health care. The amount of information you need to know, the need to make important sound judgments constantly, and the stressful work environments in our professions can easily become overwhelming. You may hear colleagues, friends, and family members encouraging you to practice self-care, to detach, or to leave your work at the hospital or clinic. They mean well, but, in the long run, they are wrong. You don't want to create two lives as you live out your faith in Jesus Christ. It will not sustain you. Your work and your personal life will suffer. You will likely experience burnout, take it out on others, or just withdraw into survival mode getting through one more shift at a time. More importantly, you will not align yourself with all that God wants to do through you at the front lines. A robust prayer life will renew your strength and courage as you practice by faith, unashamed of the gospel.

Prayer confirms and reinforces your faith in the Lord. Use prayer to praise his wisdom, his goodness, and his power. Use it to bring your thoughts, feelings, and concerns to God. Trust that he hears you, cares for you, and wants what is ultimately best for you. Jesus tells us that God knows what you need before you ask him (Matt 6:8). Think of your prayer time as an opportunity to tell God that you believe what Jesus says. Also think of your prayer time as where God increases your trust in him.

A robust prayer life involves consistency, time, and posture. Keep it simple. Spend time with God in the Bible every day. Spend time with him in prayer every day. Pray with a posture that communicates an attitude of dependence on the Lord, knowing that the mediation of Jesus Christ and the intercession of the Holy Spirit makes our prayers effective.

There are no gimmicks or special formulas for spending time in prayer with God. Angie, for example, prays at the beginning, in the middle, and at the end of her days. She begins her days before 6:00 a.m. reading Scripture verses she leaves on her bathroom vanity. She then goes into her sitting room to complete her daily Bible reading plan. She then spends time in prayer. Throughout her days at the clinic, she prays for patients by name as she washes her hands before taking care of them. Before going to sleep, she finishes her day reading a devotional and in prayer. Michael's prayer life is a bit different. He considers his mornings the primary time for him to be alone with God. After finishing his morning Bible reading, he goes to the same spot in the corner of his bedroom to pray on his knees. At this point, Jason still has younger children in the home, so his prayer time will often include them. He begins his day alone on the back porch with Bible reading and prayer. Before his kids head off to school, the family has a brief Bible reading, devotional thought, and then praying together. The kids' day often ends with a gospel-centered conversation with Jason or his wife, Kimberly, and prayer time before bed. Kimberly is Jason's favorite prayer partner.

Give yourself permission to find what works for you. The amount of time or the number of times of prayer in a day is not the key question. The important thing is that you make prayer a priority in your life because your loving Father listens and acts.

Strategy #3: Practice Sabbath Rest

Health-care professionals practice in stressful workplace settings. These settings emphasize long hours, productivity, and performing well under demanding conditions. As a CHP, you are susceptible to engaging in over-functioning. Over-functioning occurs when you rely on yourself to persevere and survive. It happens when you push your mind and body to work too hard for too long with too little rest. Over-functioning is counterproductive as it will result in you practicing health care with less patience, more fatigue, and more anxiety. Additionally, other areas of your life will suffer. You will feel so exhausted that you will have little bandwidth to love family and friends well. Your relationship with God will suffer as you will avoid reading his Word and being in prayer. It is very difficult to thrive on the front lines when you over-function. Practicing Sabbath rest can help.

Practicing Sabbath rest is the antidote to over-functioning. God created the Sabbath and made it holy. God created heaven and earth in six days. He then rested on the seventh day and commanded the Israelites to keep it holy by not working on that day (Gen 2:1–3; Exod 20:8–11). Sabbath rest is different from just taking time off or going on a vacation, although those things are important for you to thrive and endure as well. Rather, practicing Sabbath rest involves regularly stepping away from the world and spending time with the Lord. Jesus engaged in Sabbath rest. For example, after healing many people who were sick with various diseases and casting out demons, he awoke early the next morning to go to a desolate place to pray

(Mark 1:29–36). Then right before his betrayal and arrest, Jesus went away from his disciples and fell on his face and prayed (Matt 26:36–46).

One striking difference between a Sabbath rest and its secular counterparts is that the time is focused on the Lord and not just your personal recovery or physical/mental rest. The book of Hebrews provides the most explicit teaching on the Christian's Sabbath rest. Hebrews 3 and 4 contain a long interaction with Psalm 95 as a warning on missing out on God's rest. Hebrews 4:9 is the only NT verse that uses the term for Sabbath rest (*sabbatismos*), and its context in the book of Hebrews helps us see that this rest is corporate as well as individual. The Old Testament saints longed for this rest, which was to be found in a heavenly city built by God rather than an earthly resting place or city (11:10, 16; 12:22). The heavenly city, the perfect rest, is a joyful gathering of God's people who are rejoicing in his glorious work on their behalf through the mediator of a new covenant, Jesus (12:22–24). As New Testament scholar F. F. Bruce says in his commentary on Hebrews, "an experience which they do not enjoy in their present mortal life, although it belongs to them as a heritage, and by faith they may live in the good of it here and now."[1] Sometimes our closest experience of this future hope and rest that Hebrews describes is the gathering of believers each week for corporate praise, preaching of the Word, and sharing in Communion as the remembrance of the work of our High Priest, Jesus (Heb 10:19–25). As we worship together, we long for that perfect Sabbath rest promised in Jesus.

The tools that the biblical author explains that God has provided to protect believers from missing this rest are to "encourage one another day after day" to protect each other from a hardened heart and unbelief (3:12–19), listening to the preached Word with ears of faith (4:1–10), responding to God's Word with obedience (4:11–13), and drawing near to God in prayer and worship through the door that Christ, our High Priest, has opened for

---

[1] F. F. Bruce, *The Epistle to the Hebrews*, rev. ed. (Grand Rapids: Eerdmans, 1990), 110.

us (4:14–16). The writer of Hebrews is encouraging perseverance in faith so that we do not miss the promised rest that will come, in the future, when we can be like God and rest from our work also. Revelation 14:13 describes this future rest, "Then I heard a voice from heaven saying, 'Write: Blessed are the dead who die in the Lord from now on.' 'Yes,' says the Spirit, 'so they will rest from their labors, since their works follow them.'"

We believe Sabbath rest is beneficial for all believers. We encourage you to consider it an important spiritual discipline for CHPs. Why? Because practicing Sabbath rest emphasizes faith in God and serves as a reminder of your limitations. Sabbath rest also reinforces the right order in your relationship with God. He is God. You are not. He is sovereign over all his creation. He is sovereign over your life and your health-care practice. Sabbath rest will help you abide in him, finding encouragement in his Word, through solitary prayer and through his body (the church), instead of striving to make it on your own.

Strategy #4: Perspective on the Harvest and the Work

Practicing health care while abiding in Christ is the right perspective for CHPs. We serve God as his ambassadors on the front lines. Our tasks are diverse, much like tilling the soil, cultivating an environment conducive to sharing the gospel with words and actions. At times we repair and restore. At times we admonish. At times we may explicitly share the gospel of grace. At other times we may implicitly testify to God's love as we care for patients and colleagues as servants of common grace. Remember, however, it is God who saves. Though he does not need us, he allows us to participate in the reconciliation ministry, in the harvest. The words of Jesus in John 15 provide both encouragement and warning. Abide in him and you will bear much fruit. Apart from him, you can do nothing (John 15:5). Steer your health-care practice away from self-reliance, or even worse, self-glorification. Place your work and your place in the harvest firmly on your dependence upon your relationship with Jesus Christ.

Strategy #5: Find Brother-in-Christ or Sister-in-Christ Relationships

It is essential to develop brother-in-Christ or sister-in-Christ relationships in health care. You need to have relationships with people who share the same commitment to glorifying Jesus Christ in every facet of their practice. Consider cultivating an intentional relationship with one or two people and a small group with other CHPs. There will be times and subjects more suited to an intimate discussion with one or two people, and other times and subjects where a small group can be helpful. Depending on the size and location of your church (and its proximity to your workplace), it may be that these relationships are first fostered in your local church body and could be an extension of the gospel fellowship that is central to healthy churches.

Brother-in-Christ or sister-in-Christ relationships offer you more than friendship. They will become your place for support, encouragement, and loving admonishment (Col 3:15–17). These are the people with whom it is safe to be vulnerable. When the challenges of practice become overwhelming, these are the friends and mentors who will truly understand. Having trusted confidants who not only understand but live out the same calling becomes an invaluable asset for spiritual growth and endurance. These relationships provide a safe space to discuss experiences, seek guidance, and learn from each other through the transformative lens of Scripture. Spend time fostering such relationships so you will have a network of CHPs providing unwavering support as you walk together in the pursuit of glorifying Jesus Christ in every situation you encounter in practice.

Strategy #6: Engage in Christian Fellowship

Foster relationships that will allow you to participate in Christian fellowship. Yes, you need brother-in-Christ or sister-in-Christ friendships with other CHPs for candid discussions about your practice. But you also need relationships outside of your work for "healthy release."

Christian fellowship encompasses more than serious discussions and theological debates. It involves the joy of shared experiences, the laughter that binds hearts, and the making of cherished memories. We believe laughter, leisure, and the creation of memories are not inconsequential pursuits; rather, they are integral to nurturing your resilience. It is also consistent with Scripture. In Mark 6:31, Jesus advised his disciples to rest after their laborious ministry endeavors, acknowledging the necessity of physical and spiritual revitalization. In a similar vein, Paul found comfort and renewal through the believers who greeted him on his way to Rome (Acts 28:11–16). King Solomon reminds us, there is "a time to weep, and a time to laugh; a time to mourn, and a time to dance" (Eccl 3:4). He also writes, "A joyful heart is good medicine, but a crushed spirit dries up the bones" (Prov 17:22).

The apostle Paul points to the local church as the central place to establish Christian fellowship. Our fellowship is then fashioned around the wisdom of God, the preaching of the gospel, and the authoritative teaching of God's Word. In 1 Corinthians 11–14 Paul instructs the church at Corinth at length about corporate habits that either build up or tear down Christian fellowship. He provides instructions on communion so that it remains a corporate remembrance of Christ and not just an individual act (1 Cor 11:26–27, 33). He writes about using spiritual gifts for the sake of the whole body "so that there would be no division in the body, but that the members would have the same concern for each other" (12:25). He encourages members of the church to look to God's provision of church leaders who will lead and serve the body (12:27–31). Paul also speaks about how Christian fellowship unites us in the hard moments and trying seasons as well as on the occasions for rejoicing and celebration. He speaks of the local church as having such strong Christian community that "if one member suffers, all the members suffer with it; if one member is honored, all the members rejoice with it" (12:26).

Engage in Christian fellowship as a form of soul care. Allow yourself permission to "have fun" and nurture a joyful heart in the light of God's love. Celebrate life moments together with other believers. Sing God's praises together, loudly. Shout with joy when a new believer is baptized. Clap in agreement when people testify to God's amazing grace. Embrace opportunities for joyful fellowship just as you do opportunities for demonstrating joyful obedience. God can use both to shape you more and more into his effective vessel of healing.

Strategy #7: Consider Local and/or Global Missions

Nurturing a deeper relationship with Jesus Christ should be at the core of all that you do. But serving full-time on the front lines is demanding. It is easy to begin feeling consumed by the hustle and bustle of where you practice as well as by the demands on your personal life. Mission work offers juncture points to bring together your expertise in health care with the explicit focus of sharing your faith. Just as important, volunteering with local and/or global missions is an act of surrendering every facet of existence to Christ where you manifest the words of John the Baptist when he says, "He must increase, but I must decrease" (John 3:30). Growing in spiritual maturity helps sustain you in practice every day at the hospital, agency, or clinic. Engaging in God's work of missions can stretch you and give you new opportunities for spiritual growth. Spiritual maturity and an awareness of God's global purposes enable you to see your role in health care within the larger context of God's plan.

Your calling as a CHP extends far beyond the confines of medical institutions and clinics. The words of Jesus are for everyone who calls him Lord and Savior. He said to his disciples:

> "All authority has been given to me in heaven and on earth. Go, therefore, and make disciples of all nations, baptizing them in the name of the Father and of the Son and of the Holy Spirit, teaching them to observe everything I have commanded you. And remember, I am with you always, to the end of the age." (Matt 28:18–20)

This commission to original disciples extends to us today. Additionally, Jesus acknowledged the differing areas of ministry that his disciples would have when he said, right before ascending to heaven, "You will be my witnesses in Jerusalem, in all Judea and Samaria, and to the end of the earth" (Acts 1:8). Being a witness beginning in our neighborhood and extending to the nations is not just a call for pastors and career missionaries. These verses point to a divine mandate and opportunity to learn to see your service in health care as part of the Great Commission.

This is another amazing blessing about how God works. As you step out in faith to serve on missions, the Lord can transcend your service to reinvigorate you for the work locally. I (Jason) have known CHPs in my church who have said that an annual "medical missions" trip changed their viewpoint of the value of their training. About three decades ago, I heard regularly from a dentist friend that his dental work paired with evangelistic conversations on his trips to South America made the weekly grind worth it.

Angie and I (Michael) know from experience that some CHPs practice in work environments that are exceedingly difficult. The unit, the people, the administration, and the ongoing staff shortages can make every shift a struggle. The reality is you may work somewhere that will not get better. Things may always seem toilsome. Still, for whatever reason, you just do not feel at peace about leaving. You just know the Lord has you there representing him as his ambassador. If this is you, then know that the Lord can use your participation in missions to infuse new life into your daily routines, helping you see your Jerusalem with a more profound sense of purpose. In other words, God can use the anticipation of mission work and the experiences of mission work to help you thrive and endure, even if the external circumstances at work never seem to change. What *will* change is you. God will use your mission work to give you a fresh perspective, a renewed energy, and a revitalized spirit as you remain steadfast in joyful obedience, caring for patients and colleagues as a servant of common grace.

You Are Not Alone: Help from Above

Pray as Jesus taught us:

> *"Our Father in heaven, your name be honored as holy.*
> *Your kingdom come. Your will be done on earth as it is in heaven.*
> *Give us today our daily bread.*
> *And forgive us our debts, as we also have forgiven our debtors.*
> *And do not bring us into temptation, but deliver us from the evil one."*
> (Matt 6:9–13)

NAME AND SUBJECT INDEX

A

Abednego, 53–54
Abraham, 36–37, 39, 94–95. *See also* covenant: Abrahamic; Hagar; Sarah
abuse, 20, 23, 108, 110, 115, 124
Adam and Eve. *See also* covenant: Adamic
  curse of, 20–21
  disobedience of, 21, 34, 65–66
  and eternal life, 34
  purpose of, 64
addiction, 1, 72. *See also* substance abuse
agony, 94, 103
Aikens, Judy, 13–14, 16–17, 28
alcoholism, 108
Alypius (friend of Augustine), 103. *See also* Augustine: Confessions
ambassadorship, 5–6, 170, 178–79, 185. *See Chapter 8, "Ambassadorship,"* 167–85
Ambrose of Milan, 102
American Academy of Physician Assistants, 23
American Medical Association, 22
American Nurses Association, 22
American Physical Therapy Association, 22
American Society of Radiologic Technologists, 22
Ananias (biblical figure), 160
anesthesia, 85, 133, 169–70
angel of the Lord, the, 99–100
animosity, 69, 97, 120–21, 160
antipsychotics, 108, 120. *See also* hallucinations; paranoia
anxiety, 21, 62, 79, 103, 121, 192
Aquinas, Thomas, 18
Aristotle, 18
ascension, the, 5, 24, 47, 180
assurance, 5, 46, 90, 163–64, 177
athletic trainer, 17, 20, 23, 150–51, 179, 189
Atlas of Human Anatomy, 75
Augustine of Hippo, 27, 102–4, 125–27. *See also* Alypius; Monica
  On Christian Doctrine, 27, 126
  Confessions, 102–4

B

Baal, 96. *See also* Elijah
Babylon, 53–54
Barnett, Melissa, 129–32, 137–38, 141–42
Barnett, Paul, 135
Basil of Caesarea, 145–46
Beeman, Adilynn, 107–8, 110–11, 115, 120–21
Bipolar I Disorder, 160
boldness, 89, 142
Borderline Personality Disorder, 160
breath of life, the, 21, 72, 171
brokenness, 5, 123, 144, 152–53, 155, 165–66, 183
Bruce, F. F., 193
burnout, 1, 6, 60, 62, 75, 79, 89, 101, 114, 143, 183, 188, 191

C

calling, divine, 1–2, 23–24, 63, 102, 174, 189, 195, 197–98
Calvin, John, 164–65
Canaan, 53
cancer, 13–14, 30
Carson, Pam, 14–17, 19, 28
Celsus, 25
cervical fusion, 169
chaos, 18, 36, 71, 113, 120, 137, 164
child protective services, 30–31
chronic pain, 94
Chrysostom, John, 26
church, joining a, 77
codes of ethics, 17, 22–23, 28, 73, 124, 171
comfort, 3, 5, 21, 47, 51, 59, 84–105, 107, 111–16, 121, 125, 130, 132, 138, 173–74, 177, 196. *See Chapter 4, "Comfort,"* 85–105.
common grace. *See Chapter 3, "Servants of Common Grace,"* 57–82
- in the Bible, 64–71
- definition of, 3, 63–64
- evidence of, 70–71
- as free gift, 66
- purposes of, 71–74
- scope of, 52–54

compartmentalization, 3, 62, 111
compassion, 22–24, 27, 50, 92, 116
condemnation, 35, 107–8, 115, 117, 119, 134–35
confession, 5, 180, 188
conscience, 46, 71–72, 125, 175
contemplation. *See* meditation
contempt, 26, 36, 94, 162, 165
Cooksey, Breanna, 150–52
Corinth, 50, 83–84, 112, 135, 154, 196
covenant
- Abrahamic, 36–39, 41
- Adamic, 33–34
- Davidic, 38–41
- Mosaic, 37–38, 40–41, 50, 134
- New, 39–41, 45, 47, 50–51, 54–55, 134–36, 193
- Noahic, 35–36, 66–68

COVID-19, 12, 57–59, 149. *See also* isolation
credentials, 132, 136, 143, 154, 178
credibility, 178

D

Damascus, road to, 87, 154
Daniel (prophet), 53–54
David (king), 19, 38–40, 105, 116, 180

death of Christ, 6, 43, 47, 118, 162
decisions, bad, 4, 20, 96, 110, 124, 127
dentist, 179, 198
depravity, 1, 52
depression, 21, 62
destructive behavior, 114
devotion, 59, 63
diagnosis, 21, 31
Diagnostic and Statistical Manual of Mental Disorders, 75
dignity, 22–23, 165
DiSalvo, Lloyd, 149–50, 152, 159
discipleship, 7, 60–62, 75–77, 101, 113
discomfort, 20–21, 31, 86
discord, 120
discouragement, 95–96
disobedience, 21, 23, 33, 39–40, 64–66, 135
distress, 3, 88–89, 92, 95–99, 101, 182
division, 113, 196
Down syndrome, 151–52

E

Eden, garden of, 20, 35, 64–66
Edwards, Jonathan, 51–54
Egypt, 53, 94, 99
Elijah (prophet), 96–97. *See also* Baal
Elisha (prophet), 97
empathy, 93, 110
Esau (biblical figure), 31–32
eternal life, 5
  access to, 32–34
  and Jesus, 44–45, 54, 68, 87, 102, 119, 125, 157, 181
Evans, Dan, 169–70, 172, 174
evil influences, 166
exhaustion, 21, 75, 97, 152, 192
expertise, 6, 59, 93, 154, 170, 174, 178, 190, 197

F

faith alone, 5, 70, 164
faith and science, intersection of, 25
fall, the, 21, 34–35, 110, 136
Faye, Lisa, 11–12, 16–17, 19, 28
flight nurse, 129–30, 137
forgiveness, 4–5, 24, 38–40, 43, 45, 48, 50, 54, 84, 91, 102, 173–74, 177, 199. *See Chapter 5, "Forgiveness,"* 107–28
freedom, 119, 127, 142–43

G

gastrocnemius, 99
Gentiles, 24, 37, 46, 71
geriatrics, 12, 21, 171
glory, permanent, 5–6, 84, 133–40, 143–44, 147, 152, 154, 162, 174, 177, 185
Good Samaritan, parable of, 105
grace alone, 5, 70, 164
Great Commission, the, 198
grief, 4, 21, 96–97, 107, 111–15, 119–21, 123–24, 137, 141
grievances, 117, 160

H

Hagar (biblical figure), 94–95
hallucinations, 107–8, 115. *See also* antipsychotics; paranoia
Harris, Murray, 89
hell, 108
helplessness, 5, 85–86, 94, 133, 147
Hezekiah (king), 80
Hodgkin lymphoma, 132
Holy Spirit, the, 4–6, 24, 47–49, 62, 73–74, 76, 78–79, 81, 89,

91, 104, 136, 139, 144, 148, 153–54, 162, 166, 173, 180–81, 187–89, 191, 197
homelife, 23, 171
hospice, 131–32, 138, 146
humility, 76, 121, 126, 157, 164–65, 189

I

identity, 9, 46, 83, 117, 120, 164
idolatry, 53–54
idols, 71, 181, 184
incontinence, 13
insurance companies, 15, 79, 101
integration, 28, 62–63, 122, 144, 167, 172, 188
internship, 61, 133
invitation of God, 79–80, 93
Isaac (biblical figure), 37
isolation, 58–59. *See also* COVID-19

J

Jacob (biblical figure), 31–32, 37, 53, 96
Jewish people, 24, 44, 46, 53, 180
John the Baptist, 44, 69, 197
Joseph (biblical figure), 53, 96–97
Joshua (biblical figure), 53, 79
joy, 86, 118–19, 122–25
    in Christ, 121
    eternal, 164
    amid pain, 5–6, 16, 59, 62
    and Satan, 4
    amid stress, 86, 100
    temporary, 72
joyful obedience, 139, 142, 144, 153–55, 158, 162–63, 172, 178, 180, 188, 197–98
Joyner-Williams, Tanya, 15–17, 19
judgment, divine, 32
justice, 39–40, 66, 71, 119

K

Kruse, Colin, 163

L

Last Supper, the, 99–100
laughter, 196
leisure, 196
Lord's Prayer, the, 199

M

Malachi (prophet), 32
mammography, 13–14
Martin, Ralph, 177
mediator, 40, 45, 81, 193
meditation, 77–78, 140
memories, 14, 196
mental health, 5, 93, 101, 107, 115, 149, 152, 160
mental illness, 110
Mephibosheth, 105
mercy, 54, 66, 120, 123
    of God, 36, 87–88, 103, 126, 141, 159
    and grief, 4
    infinite, 119
    of Jesus, 24
    sharing of, 119
    work of, 27
Meshach, 53–54
misery, 94, 98
missions, 7, 16, 97, 197–99
Monica (mother of Augustine), 102–4, 126
Morgan, Jane, 151–53
mortality, 3, 17, 20–21, 23, 28, 52, 72, 126, 129, 137, 158, 171–72, 176, 183

Moses, 37, 40, 42–44, 49–50, 53, 79, 134, 179–80. *See also* covenant: Mosaic

N

National Association of Social Workers, 22
National Athletic Trainers' Association, 23
natural birth, 18
Nebuchadnezzar, 54
nephrologist, 30–31
new creation, 173, 175, 177
new life, 39, 48–49, 90, 173, 188–89, 198
Noah. *See* covenant: Noahic
nurse anesthetist, 169–70, 172
nursing assistant, 12, 17, 86–87

O

oath, 22–23, 28, 73, 124, 171
obedience, 34, 53, 79, 117–18, 135, 193
  and forgiveness, 117–18, 123
  joyful, 139, 142, 144, 148, 153–54, 158, 162–63, 172, 178, 180, 188, 197–98
  and the Mosaic covenant, 38
  of Noah, 35
  and the Spirit, 47, 78–79, 135
oncology, 30, 132
Origen, 25
original sin, 52. *See also* Edwards, Jonathan

P

palliative care, 21, 132
paperwork, 14, 93, 101
paradox, 9–10, 157, 162
paranoia, 108, 115. *See also* antipsychotics; hallucinations
Passover, 99–100
patience, 76, 87, 100, 104, 110, 116, 123, 125, 192
pectus carinatum, 30
pediatrics, 21, 85, 171
peripheral neuropathy, 30
persecution, 5, 57, 155, 160–61, 166
perseverance, 121, 125, 162–63, 166, 190, 192, 194
Peter (apostle), 48, 123, 181
physical therapist, 12, 17, 20, 22, 108–10, 179
physician assistant, 17, 20, 23, 85–86, 167–68, 171, 179. *See also* American Academy of Physician Assistants
Physicians' Desk Reference, 75
poetic books, 49
posture, 4, 6, 191
powerlessness, 4–5, 96
prayer, 6, 54–55, 76–77, 184–85, 190–94
  and access to God, 173
  answers to, 92
  confessional, 117
  daily, 130
  of Jesus, 48
  persistent, 104
pregnancy, 12, 94
presence of God, 46, 72
prime mover, 17–18, 22
Promised Land, the, 38, 40, 179
providence, 164–65
psychiatrist, 108, 120, 149–50
psychosomatic symptoms, 30–31
pulmonologist, 30–31

R

race, 23–25, 74, 171, 188
recent convert, 28, 62
reconciliation, 175, 177, 183, 194
repentance, 5, 35, 43, 46, 112
restoration, 4, 72, 98, 113, 137, 156, 174
resurrection, 91, 157
  future, 163
  hope of, 26, 90
  implications of, 43
  of Jesus, 5, 42–44, 47, 141, 162, 180
  and the Spirit, 48
road to Emmaus, the, 42
Rose, Emily, 86–87
Russell, Corey, 108–11, 115, 120–21

S

Sabbath rest, 6, 192–94
safety, 23, 85, 130
Salentiny, Keith, 12–13, 16–17, 28
Samaritans, 24
sanctification, 76
Sarah (biblical figure), 37, 94–95
Satan, 4, 66, 112–13, 120–21
Scaglione, Paul, 131–32, 137–38, 142, 147
schizophrenia, 107, 115
self-glorification, 194
self-medication, 143
self-reliance, 194
sexual assault, 30
sexual orientation, 23, 171
Shadrach, 53–54
Shema, the, 179–82
sin, consequences of, 3–4, 66, 68, 110–11, 113, 124
social class, 23, 171
social worker, 9–10, 13–15, 17, 21–22, 30, 63, 91, 131–32, 138, 179, 185, 189
solidarity, 77
Solomon (king), 196
Son of David. *See* covenant: Davidic
sorrow, 4, 21, 112, 115–16, 158
sports medicine, 151
Spurgeon, Charles Haddon, 182–83
status
  faith, 64
  of ministers, 164
  new, 177
  professional, 154
  socioeconomic, 23
stewardship, 2, 5, 36, 50
stress, 20, 62, 82, 86, 97, 100, 118, 143, 163, 170, 190, 192. *See also* self-medication
struggle, 3, 100, 198
substance abuse, 5. *See also* addiction
suffering. *See Chapter 7, "Jars of Clay,"* 149–66
sufficiency of God, the, 133, 138, 174, 177–78
sufficiency of the Bible, the, 2
suicidal ideation, 1
surgery, 15, 85, 109, 150, 169, 172

T

telehealth, 12
Tertullian, 80–81
Therapeutic Modalities for Musculoskeletal Injuries, 75
Thompson, Shelly, 57–61, 78
Tolley, Harris, 132, 138, 142, 147
transfiguration, the, 181
trauma, 109, 129, 131, 133, 137, 155

childhood, 120
processing of, 20
vicarious, 1
tree of life, the, 18, 32, 34, 65

U

unbelief, 47–48, 51, 54–55, 69, 72, 136, 178, 193

V

vulnerability, 5, 14, 19, 94, 149, 170, 172, 176, 195

W

Walking Dead, The, 137
welfare, 23
well-being, 3, 22–23, 73, 93, 97, 119–20, 174
overall, 81, 95–96, 111, 113
permanent, 136
temporal, 5
Wells, Brenda, 29–31
Whitworth, Ian, 85–86
wholeness, 72
wilderness, 53, 94, 97
wisdom, 33, 42, 76, 79, 126, 130, 147, 188
of God, 33, 79, 126, 140, 191, 196
of Jesus, 47
from Scripture, 49, 75
of the serpent, 126
Woodburn, Sydney, 167–68, 170–74
wrath, 70

SCRIPTURE INDEX

Genesis

1 *69*
1–2 *32–33, 35*
1–3 *64*
1:26–28 *34*
1:26–31 *33*
1:28 *18*
2:1–3 *192*
2:7 *21*
2:9 *18*
2:15 *34, 64*
2:15–17 *33, 64*
2:16–17 *64*
2:17 *34*
2:24 *123*
3 *21, 32, 35*
3:14–24 *64–65*
3:15 *33–34*
3:16–19 *20*
4–5 *34*
6:3 *35*
6:5 *35*
6:6 *68*
6:8 *35*
6–9 *35*
6:17–21 *35*
6:22 *35*
8 *66*
8–9 *34*
8:20–9:17 *35, 66–67*
8:21 *35*
9:20–29 *36*
9:21–22 *36*
11 *36*
12 *36*
12:1–3 *36*
12:7 *36–37*
12–17 *36*
15:3–6 *36*
15:6 *37*
16 *94*
25 *32*
41:56 *53*
41:57 *53*
49:8–10 *38*
50 *96*
50:19–21 *96*

Exodus

11 *99*

12 *99*
19:1–9 *37*
19:3–8 *37*
19–20 *37, 50*
20 *134*
20:1–6 *38*
20:8–11 *192*
32 *38, 134*
34 *38, 49*
34:6–7 *50*
34:10 *38, 50*

Numbers

13–14 *179*

Deuteronomy

4:1–8 *37*
5 *180*
5:7–9 *181*
6 *180*
6:4–9 *179*
30 *40*
30:6–10 *40*
34:9 *79*

Joshua

1:1–18 *38*
1:6–9 *78*
21:43–45 *38*

Judges

10:13–11:27 *38*

1 Samuel

7:1–13 *38*
16–17 *19*

2 Samuel

7 *38*
7:8–17 *38*
9 *105*

1 Kings

19 *96*

1 Chronicles

17 *38*
17:10–14 *38*
17:13 *39*
17:14 *39*

Psalms

2:7 *39*
8:3–4 *180*
14:1–3 *38*
17:29 *102*
42:8 *122*
69:1 *102*
86:5 *116*
95 *193*
98:1–3 *46*
103 *142, 147*
110 *48*
119:15–16 *140*
145:8–9 *82*

Proverbs

17:22 *196*

Ecclesiastes

1–6 *133*
3:4 *196*

Isaiah

1:27–28 *46*
11 *46*
16 *46*
51:1–5 *46*

54:9–10 *36*

Jeremiah

23 *41*
23:5–6 *39*
30:3 *39*
30:9 *39*
31 *40*
31:31–34 *39–40*

Ezekiel

36 *40, 47*
36:22–32 *40*

Hosea

6:7 *34*

Habakkuk

2:4 *70*

Zechariah

7:11–12 *48*
8:7–8 *46*

Malachi

1:2–3 *32*

Matthew

1 *39*
1:21 *45*
3 *44*
4:23–24 *24*
5:14–16 *159*
5:16 *142*
6:8 *191*
6:9–13 *199*
6:33 *46*
9:2–7 *24*
9:27–29 *24*
9:35–36 *24*
9:36–38 *92*
10:19–20 *139*
10:24–25 *162*
10:29–31 *125*
11:28–30 *xv*
16:24–25 *144*
17:1–13 *181*
17:5 *181*
18:21–22 *123*
21:9 *40*
22:37–40 *122*
26:36–46 *193*
28:18–20 *197*

Mark

1:29–36 *193*
6:31 *196*
12:28–31 *185*
12:29–31 *180*

Luke

1:67–77 *41*
4:16–21 *42*
6:22 *160, 166*
10:25–37 *105*
22:14 *100*
22:19–20 *100*
24 *42, 44*
24:25–27 *42*
24:44–48 *43*

John

1 *69*
1:1–5 *68*
1:1–14 *45*
1:5 *68*
1:6–8 *69*
1:7 *44*
1:9 *68–69*

1:10–11 *69*
1:12 *44*, *69*
1:13 *69*
3:30 *197*
4:14 *102*
5 *44*
5:39–40 *44*
5:46–47 *44*
7:37–39 *189*
8:23–24 *189*
11:33–36 *24*
13 *47*
13:1–20 *100*
14 *47*
14:2 *117*
14:6 *45*
14:15 *47*
14:15–26 *136*
14:16 *89*
14:18 *47*
14:26 *48*, *139*, *189*
15 *194*
15:1–4 *162*
15:5 *139*, *194*
15:26 *136*
16:12–15 *189*
17:20–23 *48*
17:23 *48*

Acts

1:8 *198*
5:12–14 *24*
8:4–8 *24*
9 *154*
9:15–16 *160*
14:8–17 *25*
14:16–17 *82*
17:1–13 *25*
28:11–16 *196*

Romans

1 *70*
1–4 *47*
1:17 *70*
1:18–23 *70*
1:19–20 *6*
2 *71*
2:14–15 *70–71*
3:10–12 *38*
3:20 *70*
4:9–14 *37*
5:8 *6*, *117*
6:5–11 *180*
6:16–18 *117*
7:13 *134*
8 *47*
8:1 *117*
8:8–11 *189*
8:11 *48*
8:14–17 *189*
8:22–25 *189*
8:26 *48*
8:26–30 *154*
9:13 *31*
10:9 *46*
12:2 *144*
13:13–14 *103*

1 Corinthians

1–6 *112*
1:9 *45*
4:2 *xvi*
5:2 *114*
5:10–13 *114*
10:31 *146*
11–14 *196*
11:26–27 *196*
11:33 *196*
12 *49*

12:3–13 *189*
12:25 *196*
12:26 *196*
12:27–31 *196*
13:7 *1*
15:49 *154*

2 Corinthians

1 *91, 111*
1:3–7 *87, 89*
1:4 *85*
1:5–7 *90*
1:7 *100*
1:8 *88*
1:22 *91*
2 *111–12*
2:5 *112*
2:5–11 *112*
2:6 *112, 114*
2:7 *107, 114*
2:7–8 *114*
2:9 *123*
2:14–15 *122*
3 *50–51*
3:1–11 *134*
3:6 *51*
3:11 *129*
3:17–18 *154*
3:18 *144, 156–57*
4 *157*
4:5–6 *154*
4:7 *5, 149, 164*
4:7–18 *155*
4:10–12 *162*
4:10a *162*
4:14–15 *163*
4:16–18 *163*
5:4 *176*
5:5 *176*
5:7 *176*
5:9 *177*
5:10 *178*
5:11 *177*
5:11–21 *175*
5:17a *173*
5:18 *177*
5:20 *167*
6 *51*
6:4 *51*
6:4–10 *158*
6:7 *51*
9:8 *29, 51*
10:3–4a *11*
10:6 *114*
12 *51*
12:9 *51*
12:9–10 *57*
12:12 *25*
13:11 *187*
13:13 *187*

Galatians

2:20 *119, 143*
4:14 *103*
5:1 *143*
5:13–15 *143*
5:16a *79*
5:25 *79*

Ephesians

1–2 *47*
1:13–14 *48, 189*
1:17–19 *188*
2:4 *157*
3:20 *103*
4 *49*
4:3–6 *49*
4:16 *173*

4:32 *116*
5:2 *116*

Philippians

1:21 *91*
2:3 *144*
2:10–11 *48*
3:7–8 *118, 144*

Colossians

1 *45*
1:15–20 *181*
2:13–14 *119*
3:13 *114*
3:15–17 *195*

1 Timothy

1:15–16 *87*
1:16 *125*

2 Timothy

4:6 *158*

Hebrews

1:1–3 *42*
3 *193*
3:7–19 *125*
3:12–19 *193*
4 *193*
4:1–10 *193*
4:9 *193*
4:11–13 *193*
4:14–16 *194*
7:19 *135*
8–10 *40*
9:15 *40*
10 *46*
10:10 *46*
10:19–25 *193*
10:22 *46*
11:7 *35*
11:10 *193*
11–12 *41*
11:13–16 *37*
11:16 *193*
12:22 *193*
12:22–24 *193*
13:5 *160*

1 Peter

1:3–7 *141*
2:9 *74*
3:15 *142*
4:5–6 *178*

2 Peter

1:20–21 *48*
3:6–9 *35, 68*

1 John

4 *181*
4:2 *188*
4:9–11 *181*
5:13 *181*
5:14 *182*

Revelation

1:5–6 *45*
14:13 *194*
19–20 *48*
21 *48*